WILDLIFE and PLANTS of the world

An updated and expanded edition of *Wildlife of the World*

now including plants, microorganisms, and biomes

Volume 12

Marshall Cavendish
New York • London • Toronto • Sydney

Marshall Cavendish Corporation
99 White Plains Road
Tarrytown, New York 10591-9001

Created by **Brown Partworks Ltd**

Library of Congress Cataloging-in-Publication Data

Wildlife and plants of the world.
    p.   cm.
    Includes bibliographical references and index.
    Summary: Alphabetically-arranged illustrated articles introduce over 350 animals, plants, and habitats and efforts to protect them.
    ISBN 0-7614-7099-9 (set : lib. bdg. : alk. paper)
    1. Animals—Juvenile literature. 2. Plants—Juvenile literature.
[1. Animals. 2. Plants.] I. Marshall Cavendish Corporation.
    QL49.W539   1998
    578—DC21   97-32139
                                       CIP
                                       AC

ISBN 0-7614-7099-9 (set)
ISBN 0-7614-7111-1 (vol.12)

Printed in Malaysia
Bound in the United States

Brown Packaging

Editorial consultants:
- Joshua Ginsberg, Ph.D.
- Jefferey Kaufmann, Ph.D.
- Paul Sieswerda, Ph.D.
  (Wildlife Conservation Society)
- Special thanks to the Dept. of Botany, The Natural History Museum, U.K.

Editors:	Deborah Evans
	Leon Gray
Assistant editor:	Amanda Harman
Art editors:	Joan Curtis
	Alison Gardner
	Sandra Horth
Picture researchers:	Amanda Baker
	Brenda Clynch
Illustrations:	Bill Botten
	John Francis

Marshall Cavendish Corporation

Editorial director:	Paul Bernabeo
Project editor:	Debra M. Jacobs
Editorial consultant:	Elizabeth Kaplan

PICTURE CREDITS

The publishers would like to thank Natural History Photographic Agency, Ardingly, Sussex, U.K., for supplying the following pictures:
Bryan & Cherry Alexander 714, 717; A.N.T. (Bruce Thomson) 711; Anthony Bannister 720, 730; G. I. Bernard 725, 731; Joe B. Blossom 753; John Buckingham 718; Laurie Campbell 739; Stephen Dalton 746, 757, 761, 762; John B. Free 728; K. Ghani 738; Daniel Heuclin 760; E. A. Janes 742; Stephen Krasemann 715, 721, 734, 740, 741; Gerard Lacz 732, 759; Michael Leach 764, 765; Trevor McDonald 767; Dr. Ivan Polunin 755; Christophe Ratier 756; Kevin Schafer 716; John Shaw 719, 726, 727, 729, 735, 744, 745, 750, 751, 752, 763; Morten Strange 733; Karl Switak 743; Michael Tweedie 754; Bill Wood 766; David Woodfall 724.

Additional pictures supplied by:
Heather Angel 748; Ardea 749; Frank Lane Picture Agency 723, 747; Oxford Scientific Films 710, 712, 713; Planet Earth Pictures 736, 737.

Front cover
Main image: Polar bear mother and young, photographed by Stephen Krasemann.
Additional image: Cladonia bellidiflora *(lichen), photographed by Laurie Campbell.*

Status

In the Key Facts on the species described in this publication, you will find details of the appearance, name (both Latin and common name wherever possible), breeding habits, and so on. The status of an organism indicates how common it is. The status of each organism is based on reference works prepared by two organizations: *1996 IUCN Red List of Threatened Animals* published by the International Union for Conservation of Nature and Natural Resources (IUCN) and *Endangered and Threatened Wildlife and Plants* published in 1997 by the United States Government Printing Office (USGPO)

Extinct:	No sighting in the last 40 years
Endangered:	In danger of becoming extinct
Threatened:	A species that will become endangered if its present condition in the wild continues to deteriorate
Rare:	Not threatened, but not frequently found in the wild
In captivity:	A species that is extinct in the wild but has been kept successfully in captivity
Feral:	Animals that have been domesticated and have escaped into the wild
Common:	Frequently found within its range, which may be limited
Widespread:	Commonly found in many parts of the world

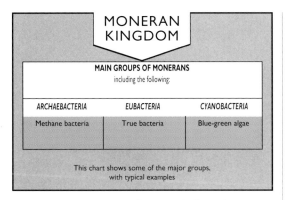

MONERAN KINGDOM

MAIN GROUPS OF MONERANS
including the following:

ARCHAEBACTERIA	EUBACTERIA	CYANOBACTERIA
Methane bacteria	True bacteria	Blue-green algae

This chart shows some of the major groups, with typical examples

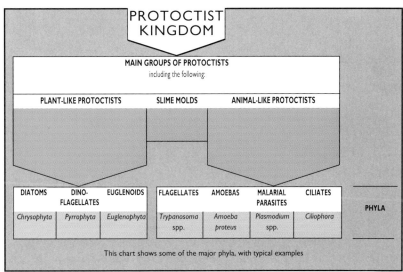

PROTOCTIST KINGDOM

MAIN GROUPS OF PROTOCTISTS
including the following:

PLANT-LIKE PROTOCTISTS			SLIME MOLDS	ANIMAL-LIKE PROTOCTISTS			
DIATOMS	DINO-FLAGELLATES	EUGLENOIDS		FLAGELLATES	AMOEBAS	MALARIAL PARASITES	CILIATES
Chrysophyta	Pyrrophyta	Euglenophyta		Trypanosoma spp.	Amoeba proteus	Plasmodium spp.	Ciliophora

PHYLA

This chart shows some of the major phyla, with typical examples

Moneran, protoctist, and fungi kingdoms

Three groups of living things are not classified in the animal and plant kingdoms. These are the moneran, protoctist, and fungi kingdoms. Monerans are tiny, single-celled organisms that have no distinct nucleus. The nucleus is the control center of the cell. In contrast, protoctists and fungi have visibly distinct nuclei and tiny organs (called organelles). However, classification is a topic for much debate, and many scientists disagree on the classification of organisms in these three kingdoms.

The moneran kingdom contains all the microscopic, single-celled organisms that do not have distinct nuclei. The three main groups of monerans are: true bacteria, blue-green algae, and methane bacteria. The largest group of monerans is the true bacteria (*Eubacteria*).

For over a billion years, bacteria were the only living things on the earth. Then about 1.5 billion years ago, new organisms, called protoctists (formerly known as protists), evolved from the methane bacteria. All protoctists are single-celled organisms, but their cell structure is more complex than monerans. For example, protoctists have nuclei.

Scientists tend to classify an organism as a protoctist when they cannot place the organism in the animal, plant, or fungi kingdoms. Protoctists are grouped into phyla that have animal-, plant-, or fungus-like features. Single-celled algae, such as diatoms and euglenoids, behave like plants. Amoebas can move about and are more like animals. Slime molds form a subkingdom that have characteristics similar to the fungi kingdom.

Fungi make up the last kingdom of living things. Mushrooms, toadstools, and molds are all fungi. Fungi differ from animals and plants in that they depend on other organisms for their food. Like plants, fungi form groups called divisions. There are two divisions in the fungi kingdom.

See Volume 17 for more information on monerans, protoctists, and fungi.

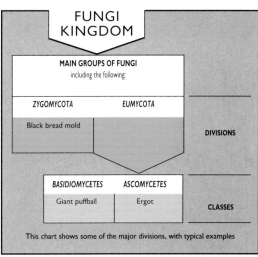

FUNGI KINGDOM

MAIN GROUPS OF FUNGI
including the following:

ZYGOMYCOTA	EUMYCOTA
Black bread mold	

DIVISIONS

BASIDIOMYCETES	ASCOMYCETES
Giant puffball	Ergot

CLASSES

This chart shows some of the major divisions, with typical examples

COLOR GUIDE

MONERANS, PROTOCTISTS, & FUNGI

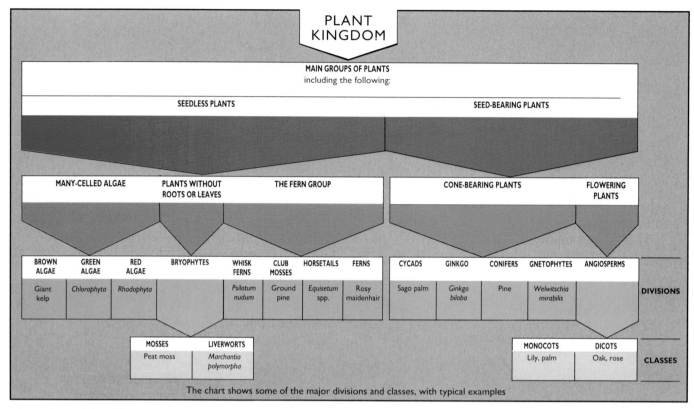

The chart shows some of the major divisions and classes, with typical examples

The plant kingdom

Every plant, from the tiniest shrub to the tallest tree, belongs to the plant kingdom. There are about 500,000 different kinds (species) of plant that have been identified.

The plant kingdom (shown above) can be divided into 13 divisions. A plant division is similar to a phylum in animal classification. Each division represents a number of classes of plants that all have certain features in common.

The simplest plants are algae, all of which live in water. This set of books classifies three divisions of multicellular (or many-celled) algae in the plant kingdom. Some scientists, though, prefer to classify multicellular algae as protoctists.

Two classes, mosses and liverworts, make up the bryophyte division. These plants lack the roots, stems, and leaves that are found in other plant divisions.

The fern group comprises four divisions of the plant kingdom: whisk ferns, club mosses, horsetails, and ferns. All members of the fern group have two stages in their life cycle. During one of these stages tiny reproductive structures, called spores, are released. These spores will eventually grow into a new plant.

More complex plants reproduce with seeds. Four divisions of plants reproduce with "naked" seeds in cones. Cycads, conifers, ginkgoes, and gnetophytes are all cone-bearing plants.

Two classes, monocots and dicots, make up the largest division of plants, the angiosperms, or flowering plants. Unlike cone-bearing plants, angiosperms reproduce with enclosed seeds such as berries, nuts, and fruits.

See Volume 17 for more information on the different divisions of plants.

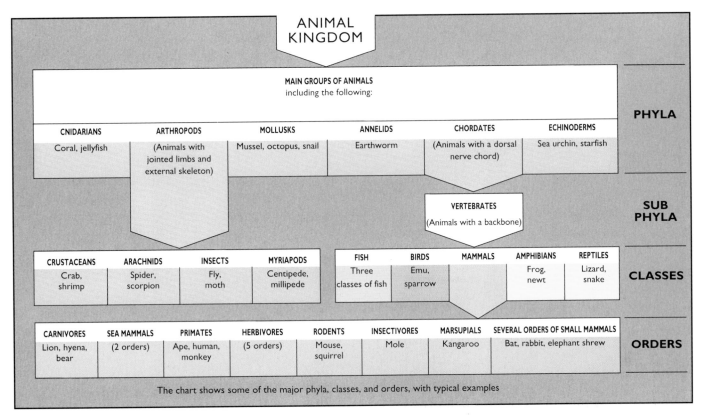

The chart shows some of the major phyla, classes, and orders, with typical examples

The animal kingdom

In the eighteenth century, a botanist from Sweden named Carl von Linné (usually known by his Latin name, *Carolus Linneaus*) outlined a system of classifying plants and animals. This became the basis for classification all over the world. Scientists use Latin names so that all plants, animals, and other living things can be identified accurately, even though they have different common names in different places. Linneaus divided living organisms into two kingdoms: plants and animals. Today most scientists divide living things into five kingdoms: animals, plants, monerans, protoctists, and fungi. The animal kingdom (*above*) is divided into many phyla. Most of the phyla of the animal kingdom contain strange creatures – microscopic organisms, sponges, corals, slugs, and insects – without the backbone and central nervous system that we associate with more familiar animals.

Each phylum is divided into classes. For example, vertebrates (animals with a backbone) are a subdivision of a phylum and are divided up into seven classes: mammals, birds, reptiles, amphibians, and three classes of fish (represented by eels, sharks, and trout).

Each of these classes is broken down further into different orders. The mammal class, for instance, includes the orders carnivores (meat eaters), insectivores (insect eaters), primates (monkeys, apes), and marsupials (kangaroos, koalas), among others.

In this set of books, we give Latin names for different groups (genera) and kinds (species) of animals. See Volume 17 for more information on the different phyla of animals.

COLOR GUIDE

INVERTEBRATES

FISH

AMPHIBIANS & REPTILES

BIRDS

MAMMALS

PLANTS

BIOMES & HABITATS

MONERANS, PROTOCTISTS, & FUNGI

Platypus

KEY FACTS

● **Name**
Platypus or
Duck-billed platypus
(*Ornithorhynchus
anatinus*)

● **Range**
Eastern Australia,
from Queensland
to Tasmania

● **Habitat**
Streams and rivers
with banks suitable
for burrows

● **Appearance**
17-24 in (45-60 cm)
long including bill and
tail; the bill is about
$2^1/_2$ in (5.5 cm) long;
the tail is 3-5 in
(8.5-13 cm); dark
brown with a paler
underside; dense fur;
sharp claws and
webbed toes

● **Food**
Invertebrates,
particularly at the
larval stage

● **Breeding**
Usually 2 soft-shelled
eggs, laid in a nesting
chamber in a long
burrow; incubated by
the female; the young
feed on milk from
mammary patches

● **Status**
Rare

The platypus is one of the strangest mammals in the world. Indeed, when the first dried skins were brought to Europe from Australia at the end of the eighteenth century, some scientists thought they must be fakes. The skin was about the same size as an otter, but the creature had a beak like a duck and leathery webbing between its toes.

When scientists found out more about the platypus, they realized that its breeding methods were even stranger than its looks. Like birds and reptiles, the platypus lays eggs. The only other mammals to do this are the two species of echidna (which were unknown at the time when platypuses were discovered).

▲ *Platypuses are strong swimmers, using their front paws to "pull" themselves through the water and steering with their back paws.*

Swimming for food

The platypus lives along the banks of rivers and streams down the eastern part of Australia and in Tasmania. It is found in a wide range of different environments, from cool mountain streams to sluggish tropical rivers. Platypuses have two layers of thick fur to provide waterproofing and insulation as they swim in search of food. When they dive under water, they have to close their eyes and ears, but their bills are very sensitive so they can feel for food on the riverbeds. (When the first platypus skin was brought to Europe, it was dried so the bill seemed hard like that of a duck. In fact, the bills are quite supple and leathery.) Platypuses feed almost entirely on invertebrates – insects and the like – and they seem to prefer them when they are at the larval stage, creeping on the bottom. They compete with some large fish for food, although most fish catch their prey when it is older and able to swim rather than when it is living on the bottom of their underwater habitat. Platypuses have flattened tails, rather like those of beavers, and these act as a fat store so that they can build up supplies for times when there is little food about.

Under water and underground

The feet and tails also play an important part in platypuses' breeding behavior. Female platypuses dig complex tunnels, which is why they need claws; they roll the webbed skin back from their toes to expose the claws. The tunnels may be long and complex, with several nesting chambers. Platypuses mate under water, and after mating the female lays two eggs (occasionally one or three). She stays in the nesting chamber to keep them warm, holding them between her tail and her stomach. The eggs are soft with leathery shells, smaller than a table-tennis ball.

It is about 10 days before the eggs hatch. The young are very poorly developed, and creep through the mother's fur to find her mammary patches. She does not have teats like other mammals, but she produces milk that collects on her fur for the young to suck. The young platypuses stay in their burrow for about three months, until they

▲ *Although they spend much of their time under water, platypuses do come out of rivers and waddle over rocks. Indeed, they lay their eggs out of the water in burrows. The female takes great care of her offspring, but does not breed every year.*

are old enough and strong enough to learn to swim and forage for themselves.

Protection

At the beginning of the twentieth century platypuses were nearing extinction. They were hunted for their fur, their meat – and their novelty value. Since laws were passed to protect them, their numbers have increased again. However, it is important that humans do not upset the natural balance of their habitats if they are to survive.

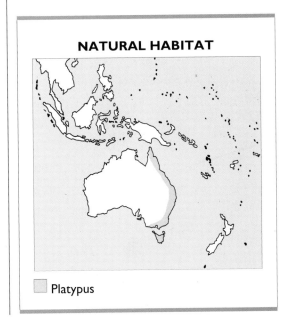

NATURAL HABITAT

Platypus

Pocket gopher

Pocket gophers are small to medium-sized rodents, with short fur and long, naked tails. They get their name from the fur-lined pockets in their cheeks, in which they carry food. There are over 30 species of pocket gopher, all of which are unique to North America. They are found from western Canada through the United States, down as far south as Mexico. However, they are not found everywhere throughout their range but occur in small, isolated areas. For example, they often live in valleys, but may not move beyond them because of the mountains that form a natural barrier restricting their spread.

Living like a mole

The pocket gopher spends most of its time beneath the ground and, like the mole, is perfectly adapted to this subterranean (underground) lifestyle. It is not blind but has very small eyes, as well as small ears, a thick body that is tapered toward the tail end, and short, strong legs.

The forelegs end in long, sharp claws that are used for digging tunnels in the earth. Rocks and compressed soil are removed with the long incisors (cutting teeth) in the upper jaw. These teeth lie outside the lips when they are closed, so that earth does not enter the gopher's mouth when it is tunneling. Its eyes produce a thick liquid substance that washes over the surface of the eyes and removes any specks of dirt that may get into them.

Pocket gophers live alone in burrows and dig tunnels of varying lengths with a

▼ *Perfectly adapted to a life digging underground, the pocket gopher has large, powerful forelimbs with long claws, a strong, sturdy body, and a naked tail that is extremely sensitive to touch and that can feel the way along the tunnels if the gopher needs to travel backward.*

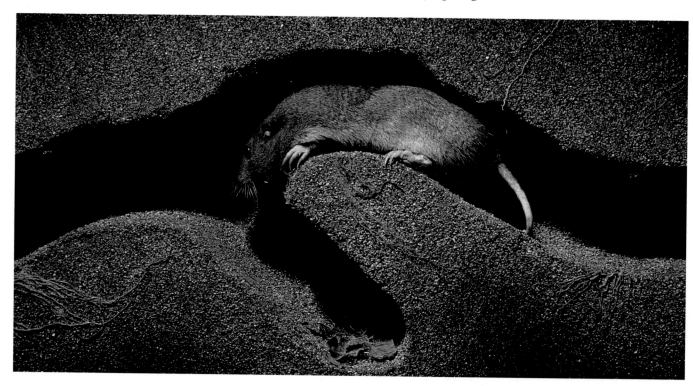

number of different rooms or chambers attached to them. These burrows often stretch a considerable distance. There are several entrances, and these can be identified by piles of earth nearby, but the entrances themselves are blocked off with soil. This deters predators from entering and maintains the correct temperature and degree of humidity (moistness in the air) inside the burrow. The gopher digs long, shallow tunnels in which it moves while gathering food, and shorter, deeper tunnels in which it shelters. There are also nesting rooms, storage rooms, and rooms used as latrines. In the northern parts of its range where there are hard, cold winters, the pocket gopher makes burrows in the snow and lines its tunnels with earth.

The gopher's tail is naked and very sensitive to the touch. The animal uses it to maneuver backward quickly through a tunnel. It arches its tail so that the tip is lifted off the ground and is then in a position to feel the way behind.

Gophers rarely leave their burrows. They do not hibernate, but they remain fairly inactive throughout the winter. They

▲ *The pocket gopher's huge incisor teeth protrude when the animal closes its lips, so that it can use them to dig without getting soil in its mouth.*

come to the surface only to find a mate, or a new place to burrow if the old one is damaged; young pocket gophers are also sometimes seen out of the burrow after they have left their mother. When they are above ground they are vulnerable to coyotes, badgers, skunks, and hawks, while snakes and weasels will hunt inside the gopher's burrow if given the chance.

Underground pantries

Gophers are so adapted to life beneath the earth that they even feed underground. They move along their tunnels searching for roots, bulbs, and tubers of plants growing through the soil. In farming areas the pocket gopher may be a pest, feeding on crops such as peas and sugar cane.

Like kangaroo rats and pocket mice, gophers place their food in their cheek pouches and carry it to a special storage room. Anything left inside the pouch can be cleaned out very easily because the gopher is able to turn the pouches inside out. Special muscles in the head pull them back into place again.

NATURAL HABITAT

Botta's pocket gopher

KEY FACTS

● **Name**
Botta's pocket gopher (*Thomomys bottae*)

● **Range**
Southwestern U.S. and northern Mexico

● **Habitat**
Underground in light, soft soil, in valleys, mountains, and coastal regions

● **Appearance**
A medium-sized rodent with a robust body measuring 4-7in (10-18 cm), with a tail of 2-3½ in (5-9 cm); small eyes and ears; large feet with long, strong claws; 4 large yellow incisor teeth and 2 fur-lined cheek pouches; the coat color varies from almost white through brown to black

● **Food**
Roots, beets, seeds, and cereal crops

● **Breeding**
About 3 weeks after mating, the female gives birth to a litter containing 2-6 young each; the newborn gophers are blind and almost completely hairless when they are born

● **Status**
Common

See also **Mole**

Polar bear

Polar bears are the largest bears in the world. Adult males may be as long as 9½ ft (3 m) from head to rump and weigh as much as 1750 lb (800 kg). They are also probably the best known members of the bear family and are easily recognizable by their white or yellowish-white coats, their long necks, and their short but sturdy limbs.

In the frozen wastes of the Arctic surrounding the North Pole, the Polar bear lives on the frozen sea. Its favorite

▲ *The Polar bear walks on the soles of its huge feet, which are covered with fur to keep them warm and stop the animal from slipping on the ice. Its hind legs are longer than its forelegs, and its back slopes down slightly from its rump to its head.*

habitat is a mixture of ice and open water. It is well protected from the bitter cold by an extra layer of insulating fat known as the subcutaneous layer, and a thick covering of warm fur. This whitish coat is also an adaptation to the Polar bear's environment because it is good camouflage in a landscape of snow and ice.

As well as walking on the ice, the Polar bear also spends some of its time in the freezing waters of the Arctic Sea. It is an excellent swimmer and can swim steadily at speeds of up to 4 mph (6.5 km/h). Its fur is waterproof and its feet are partially webbed. It uses its short, powerful forelegs to propel itself through the water, leaving its hind legs trailing along behind.

Polar bears are usually solitary animals that prefer to live and hunt alone, although they may gather together in small groups when food is scarce or much of the sea ice has melted. They are carnivores (meat eaters) that hunt for prey during the day, using their excellent sense of smell much more than their sight or hearing.

Hunting for seals

The Polar bears' favorite food is the Ringed seal, although they also hunt Bearded, Harp, and Hooded seals. These they catch by waiting patiently by holes in the ice for them to surface for breath. During April, May, and June, they use their keen sense of smell to detect seal pups in their dens up to 3 ft (1 m) under the ice. They then dig them out using their powerful forefeet and large claws.

NATURAL HABITAT

Polar bear

When seals are scarce, Polar bears also scavenge for the carcasses of walrus or whales such as narwhals, belugas, and Bowhead whales. Occasionally, if necessary, they will also catch water birds and small land mammals such as lemmings and Arctic foxes, or eat birds' eggs and available vegetation.

If they need to, Polar bears are capable of running in short bursts of up to 25 mph (40 km/h) after their prey and, once they catch it, they kill it with a powerful blow to the skull with their huge forepaws.

New life on the ice floes

Adult males and females come together during the mating season, which is in April, May, or June. Then the males become aggressive toward other rival males and go off in search of available females, which they detect by scent.

About eight months after mating, the female gives birth to one to three cubs in a special den that she has dug deep in the drifted snow along the coastline. When they are born the cubs weigh only about 0.25 percent of their mother's weight. However, their mother's milk is very high in fat, and by the time they leave the den at 4 months old they weigh 17-24 lb (8-12 kg). They remain with their mother until they are old enough to be independent at around 28 months.

▼ *This cub is old enough to leave the den and accompany its mother out into the ice and snow. It has grown substantially since it was born, when it probably weighed only 21-25 oz (600-700 g).*

KEY FACTS

● **Name**
Polar bear
(*Ursus maritimus*)

● **Range**
The Arctic, around the north pole

● **Habitat**
Coastal ice floes

● **Appearance**
The largest bear, males growing up to 9½ ft (3 m); a thick yellowish-white fur coat; a long neck; a relatively small head with small eyes and ears and a black nose; short but thick limbs with 5 claws on each broad, flat foot

● **Food**
Mainly seals; occasionally whale and walrus carcasses, small land mammals, sea birds and their eggs, vegetation

● **Breeding**
Females give birth to 1-3 cubs (usually 2) in December or January, which only weigh 21-25 oz (600-700 g) at birth; the young leave the den with their mother at about 4 months, but remain with her for another year or so

● **Status**
Widespread throughout its range

Polar regions

Earth's polar regions consist of the Arctic at the North Pole and the Antarctic at the South Pole. Together they are home to a variety of living things.

Since neither pole receives much sun they are both cold all year round. In the winter, even less sunlight together with snow mean that temperatures drop even lower. As well as being cold, it is also dry and windy so life on land is more limited than in the sea. Sometimes, however, it is warm enough for plants to grow on land and plankton to multiply in the sea. These in turn provide food for animals.

Adapting to polar life

To survive in these extreme conditions, certain species of plants and animals have adapted in various ways. During the winter some shrubs and small trees keep warm under a blanket of snow while others stop growing and produce fuzzy

▲ *A male and female Emperor penguin bow their heads as part of a courting ritual. The Emperor penguin lives in the Antarctic.*

leaves which trap water. Polar plants remain short to avoid the high winds.

Most larger animals migrate to warmer areas in the winter. Smaller species, such as invertebrates and certain mammals, sleep through the winter. The bodies of some species of fish contain a natural form of antifreeze that keeps their blood liquid as they navigate the icy waters. Large animals rely on feathers, fur, or thick layers of fat to keep them warm.

The Arctic

The Arctic is actually a group of islands covered by hundreds of feet of ice; the main group is known as Greenland. There is no land at the North Pole itself, just huge ice sheets on which only a few mosses and lichens can survive. Where there is soil, plants such as the Polar willow (*Salix polans*) grow, but only to a height of 3 ft (0.9 m). Further south, birches (genus *Betula*), grasses, and ferns can be found as well as the occasional group of wind-stunted trees such as Scots pine (*Pinus sylvestris*).

There are few spiders or insects in the soil. Flying insects as well as reptiles and amphibians are unable to survive. Only eight species of birds live in the Arctic all year round. These include Lapland buntings (*Calcarius lapponicus*) and Arctic redpolls (*Carduelis hornemanni*).

However, every summer more than 150 land species and 50 marine species migrate there. The marine species include auks and petrels, which feed on fish, insects, and

POLAR REGIONS

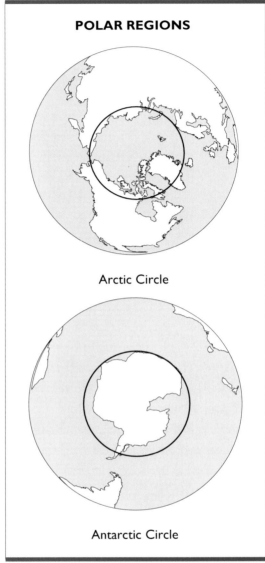

Arctic Circle

Antarctic Circle

by building shelters, and by wearing animal furs to keep warm.

The Antarctic

The Antarctic consists mainly of a single landmass with twice the surface area of Australia. It is almost entirely covered in a layer of ice that is on average just over a mile (1.6 km) thick. The Antarctic is generally colder than the Arctic.

Mosses and lichens are still found here, while other plants grow in the few areas that are free of ice. There are no resident land birds, however, and the marine birds, which include penguins, petrels, and albatrosses, survive on food from the sea.

Marine mammals such as seals, whales, and dolphins live around the coast. There are six species of seal, including the Leopard seal, which feeds on penguins. The Antarctic is the only continent on earth that has no native population of land mammals.

seeds. Only 50 mammal species are found in the Arctic. These include lemmings, shrews, voles, and in the summer, larger species such as musk oxen and caribou. Polar bears, with their thick layers of fat and fur, live in coastal areas where they hunt fish and marine mammals. Also to be found in the coastal areas is the gray wolf. In the sea over ten species of seal can be found in arctic waters, as well as walruses, whales, and narwhals.

Humans probably arrived in the Arctic 30,000 years ago and survived by hunting,

KEY FACTS

● **Location**
The Earth's polar regions consist of the Arctic at the North Pole and the Antarctic at the South Pole

● **Climate**
Extremely cold, dry and windy. Very little sunlight, especially in winter

● **Highs and lows**
Temperatures range from 5°F to 50°F (-15°C to 10°C) in the summer. In winter they are about 54°F (30°C) lower

● **Plants**
Mosses, lichens, Polar willow, Scots pine

● **Arctic animals**
Arctic redpolls, Lapland buntings, rock ptarmigan, shrews, voles, lemmings, musk oxen, and caribou. (the Antarctic has no land mammals or land birds)

◀ *The flowers and leaves of the Arctic willow (Salix arctica) are soft and furry. This helps the plant to retain water in the dry environment of the Canadian Arctic.*

See also **Lichen, Moss, Penguin, Polar bear, Seal, Walrus, Whale**

Poppy

Poppies are beautiful wildflowers with a tall, graceful stem and delicate blooms made up of large, overlapping petals. They may be white, soft pink, lilac, dark purple, bright blue, yellow, brilliant red, or orange. There are around 250 different species in the poppy family (*Papaveraceae*), most of which are found growing naturally throughout the temperate zone of the northern hemisphere. Some of the most famous are the bright red European corn poppy (*Papaver rhoeas*), the brilliant yellow Iceland poppy (*Papaver nudicaule*), the pure blue Himalayan poppy (*Meconopsis betonicifolia*), the orange Californian poppy (*Eschscholzia californica*), and the lilac-colored Opium poppy (*Papaver somniferum*).

Poppies seed themselves very easily and are often seen bringing a splash of color to derelict wasteland or fields of crops. However, they were cultivated as ornamental plants in China over 2000 years ago, and today poppies brighten up gardens in most parts of the world.

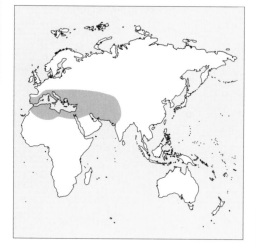

NATURAL HABITAT

Opium poppy

◀ **Opium poppy (Papaver somniferum) is a hardy, pretty wildflower that also has valuable medicinal properties.**

The life cycle of a poppy

The wide-open flowers of poppies encourage a wide range of insect visitors for pollination, including bees, beetles, hoverflies, and butterflies. They provide very rich pickings for these insects, too: one poppy plant contains as many as two and a half million grains of pollen.

The bowl-like shape of the flower allows poppies to catch as much sun as possible, especially important as they need lots of warmth for making seeds. The Arctic poppy (*Papaver radicatum*) has an additional way of ensuring that it makes the most of the brief warmth of the northern summer. As the sun moves across the sky, the poppy head moves with it, tracking the heat with its flowers.

Once a poppy has been fertilized by the pollen from another poppy flower, it sheds its petals and drops its seed. Finally, atop the stem, a dry capsule develops with a row of holes just below the top. This acts like a tiny pepper shaker, shedding the seeds as it is blown and rattled in the wind or brushed against by an animal as it passes by. The tiny, light seeds are carried on the breeze and eventually land on the ground and germinate into new poppies.

Most poppies are annuals, which means that their whole life cycle – including germination, growth, flowering, and setting seed – takes place in the space of just one year. Some species are biennials or perennials, which means that their life cycle takes two or more years to complete.

Poppy products

Many poppies have products that have been found useful to humans. For example, all species produce thick white, red, yellow, or orange latex, or resin, which is probably important for helping to close up any wounds in the plant. This resin contains a complex mixture of alkaloids that may be used in the painkillers morphine and codeine. The most famous of these drug-producing poppies is the Opium poppy, from which also comes opium, the source of the illegal drug heroin. This plant has been grown in vast numbers for its resin since ancient times, especially in China, India, Iran, Greece, and Egypt.

◀ Californian poppy (Eschscholzia californica) is an annual plant that is very easy to grow from seed.

Another very popular poppy product is the seeds, which contain delicious oils and are used widely in cooking and baking. The seeds of some species, such as Mexican poppy (*Argemone mexicana*), yield oils that are used to make soap.

A mash from the whole Opium poppy plant is used to make oil cake for cattle feed. Oil from the seeds is also employed in the manufacture of paint.

One North American species from the poppy family, *Sanguinaria canadensis*, has the common name of bloodroot because it yields a bright red sap from underground stems called rhizomes. In the past, Native Americans have used this as a dye to color the face, a treatment for sore throats and the fungal disease ringworm, a nail polish, and an insect repellent.

KEY FACTS

● **Name**
Opium poppy
(*Papaver somniferum*)

● **Range**
Probably native to the Mediterranean, naturalized in many temperate regions

● **Habitat**
Wasteland, cultivated land, and gardens

● **Appearance**
A tall wildflower, up to 3 ft (1 m) high; bluish-green stem and lobed leaves; large, bowl-shaped, pink, purple, or white flowers, often with a dark blotch at the base of each petal

● **Life cycle**
Annual

● **Uses**
Food; medicinal; ornamental

● **Status**
Common and widespread

See also **Cultivated land**

Porcupine

The porcupine is a large rodent and, despite its long spines or quills, is not related to spiny insect eaters such as hedgehogs or the echidna. Indeed, its closest relations are other cavy-like rodents such as capybaras and guinea pigs.

There are 22 species of porcupine in two distinct families: the ground-dwelling (Old World) porcupines of Africa, southern Asia, and parts of Europe, and the tree-climbing (New World) porcupines of North and South America. As well as their quills, porcupines have other distinguishing features, such as the long, chisel-like incisor teeth in both the upper and lower jaws (characteristic of all rodents). They have very poor eyesight but excellent senses of smell and hearing.

The crested porcupines (family *Hystricidae*) of Africa and southern Europe have two types of quills: short, stout ones and long, slender ones. Both are banded black and creamy white. These porcupines inhabit rocky hills with dense undergrowth. They are nocturnal and spend the day in holes in the ground or lying up among rocks. They are stocky and heavily built, and they cannot climb trees.

The tree-climbing porcupines

All of the 11 species of New World porcupines (family *Erethizontidae*) are excellent tree climbers. Their large hind feet are specially adapted for this purpose, with pads and creases on the soles and long claws on all the toes. The North American porcupine also has a well-

developed big toe on each hind foot that allows the porcupine to grasp the branches as it climbs.

Two South American groups, the Prehensile-tailed and the South American tree porcupines, use their long, spineless tails for grasping tree branches. The tip of

▼ *Crested porcupines can adapt to a wide variety of habitats, including deserts. Here they get much of their water from fruit or succulent plant roots.*

the tail curls upward and has a toughened pad of skin on the upper surface. These porcupines are the most arboreal (tree-climbing) of the New World species, spending most of their time in trees.

The North American porcupine

The North American or Canadian porcupine lives in most of the timbered areas of Canada, the United States (except the extreme southwest, southeast, and the coastal states of the Gulf of Mexico), and northern Mexico.

Its diet varies considerably from season to season. In the spring it favors the flowers and catkins of maple, poplar, and willow trees and the young green shoots of aspen and larch. During the summer months the porcupine eats herbaceous plants, and in the winter months it feeds mainly on bark, although it will also eat evergreen leaves, including those of the hemlock and pine.

As bark eaters, porcupines can do serious damage to trees, especially when they are present in large numbers. They also have a liking for corn, and several

▲ *The North American porcupine has long, silky hair hiding its short, sharp spines. This species spends much of its time on the ground but will climb high into the trees looking for food.*

individuals will quickly eat their way through a field of corn if given the chance!

Like its relatives, the North American porcupine uses its spines to ward off would-be predators. When it is threatened, it turns its arched back toward its enemy and erects its spines. The porcupine cannot "throw" its spines as people once believed, but they are so loosely held in the skin that when a predator brushes against them they become firmly embedded in its muscles. These often cause wounds that may become infected, sometimes killing the animal.

The North American porcupine's main predators are the wolverine, bobcat, puma, and fisher (a marten). The fisher is a successful porcupine hunter because it is adept at flipping the porcupine over so that the soft, spineless belly is exposed.

NATURAL HABITAT

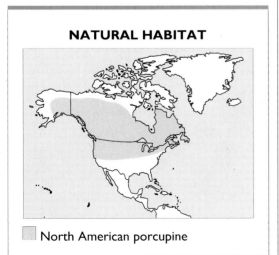

North American porcupine

Porpoise

Slender and streamlined sea mammals, porpoises are often mistaken for their close relatives the dolphins. However, they lack the typical beak-shaped face of the dolphins and have much blunter, rounder heads. Porpoises are also generally smaller than their cousins, rarely growing longer than 6 ft (1.8 m), and have smaller fins and tail flukes. Like dolphins, they belong to a group of sea mammals known as the toothed whales, which also includes white whales, beaked whales, and sperm whales.

The largest and fastest

There are six species of porpoise altogether, living in temperate waters throughout much of the world. The largest, heaviest, and probably the most easily recognized of these is the large black and white Dall's porpoise (*Phocoenoides dalli*). This porpoise is also the fastest species and may swim through the water at up to 30 mph (50 km/h).

The commonest and most widespread species is the Harbor, or Common, porpoise (*Phocoena phocoena*). Unlike many dolphins, Harbor porpoises do not usually swim in large groups. Many of them are solitary, although some may swim in pairs or small, constantly changing groups of about four individuals. They swim fairly slowly, never reaching more than about 13 mph (22 km/h), searching for prey such as fish, squid, and shrimp.

They find their prey by sight or sound, or by sending out various high- and low-pitched clicks that scan the surroundings and bounce off objects in the water, alerting the porpoises to their presence. This type of radar system is called echolocation.

Despite having up to 120 small, spade-like teeth in their jaws, porpoises do not chew their food but swallow most of it whole or tear it into large pieces.

NATURAL HABITAT

Harbor porpoise

▲ *Despite being the commonest species, the Harbor porpoise is not often seen by humans: it is able to dive for up to four minutes before coming up for air and, unlike some other species, it does not swim near boats or leap out of the water often.*

▶ *Finless porpoises (Neophocaena phocaenoides) spend most of their time in warm coastal waters around the Indian Ocean, although they often venture into rivers and estuaries around the coastline.*

Living apart for most of the year, male and female porpoises generally get together for one or two months during the summer in order to mate. About nine months later, the female gives birth to a single calf, which weighs 17½ lb (8 kg) and measures about 3 ft (1 m).

Caring for their calves without any help from the fathers, some mothers join small schools of mother-calf pairs, and they suckle their babies for between six and eight months. Once it is weaned, the calf often stays with its mother until she gives birth to a brother or sister, at which point it will leave her and become independent.

Falling numbers

Although the commonest and most widespread species in the world, the Harbor porpoise has been declining in numbers during the twentieth century due to hunting for its meat and oil, especially in the Black Sea.

It also been accidentally entangled in many modern fishing nets, as have other species such as the Burmeister's porpoise (*Phocoena spinipinnis*) and the vaquita (*Phocoena sinus*). Indeed, the vaquita (also known as the Gulf of California porpoise) is now very rare and considered by some scientists to be endangered.

KEY FACTS

● **Name**
Harbor or Common porpoise (*Phocoena phocoena*)

● **Range**
North Atlantic from West Africa to the Davis Strait and Iceland; the Black Sea; the North Pacific from southern Alaska to Baja California

● **Habitat**
Shallow coastal waters, estuaries, harbors, rivers

● **Appearance**
5½ ft (1.7 m) in length; 2 small, rounded pectoral fins, a low, triangular dorsal fin, and 2 small tail flukes; the upperparts are dark gray or black and the underparts are white or light gray

● **Food**
Herring, sardines, cod, whiting, squid, mackerel, shrimp

● **Breeding**
Females breed in the spring, once every 1-3 years; a single calf is born and suckles for 6-8 months, remaining with its mother for several months after weaning

● **Status**
Widespread

See also **Dolphin**

Potato

Baked, mashed, hash browned, french fried: it is almost impossible to imagine our diet without potatoes. Wild potato species are found from the southern United States to southern Chile, with the greatest number occuring in the Andes Mountains of South America. Wild potatoes have been a staple food in the Andes for thousands of years. Native peoples ate potatoes boiled, roasted, or raw.

The Incas of Peru widely cultivated the potato about 1500 years ago. They also dried potato tubers and stored them for winter food, or ground them into flour to make potato bread. European explorers described the potato – called "papas" by the native people – around the time of

▲ *A field of cultivated potato stretches as far as the eye can see. These healthy-looking plants are flowering.*

Columbus. By 1650, potatoes were widely grown in Ireland, where they were relished as an "excellently delicious and strongly nourishing" food.

Poison above, potato below

The potato plant (*Solanum tuberosum*) is a member of the large nightshade (*Solanaceae*) family, which contains 95 groups (genera) and at least 2400 kinds (species). Like many members of this family, such as Deadly nightshade, potato plants contain a poison in their leaves and stem. Yet we eat some potato relatives in this family, including eggplants and tomatoes. (Sweet potatoes are not real potatoes, but belong to the Morning glory family.) Remember that when potato skins turn greenish, the potatoes are turning poisonous and should be thrown away.

The potato plant is a perennial (a plant with more than one growing season). It grows to a height of 20-40 in (50-100 cm). Its 8-in (20-cm) leaves have 3-5 pairs of oval, pointed leaflets. The

HABITAT

Native range of potato

Approximate cultivated range of potato

potato plant bears several clusters of white, yellow, or purple, 1 in (3 cm) five-petaled flowers, which attract the insects that pollinate the plant.

The edible parts of the potato plant, the fleshy growths on its roots, are called tubers. They store starchy food for the plant. Each potato plant may produce from a few to 20 tubers. Every tuber develops buds, called eyes. To grow potatoes, simply cut a potato tuber into pieces that contain a bud, then plant each piece. The bud will then produce an identical potato plant.

Many variations

Cultivated potatoes come in many different sizes, shapes, and tastes, from tiny, waxy-fleshed red, round potatoes weighing only a few ounces (grams) to enormous oblong, mealy potatoes weighing up to 4 lb (2 kg) each. The potato varieties we eat most have brownish-white or brown skin.

Potato flesh is usually white (as in the baking potato or mashing potato) or yellow, but in the temperate regions around the world where potatoes are cultivated, you will find potatoes with red or purple skin and flesh. South American natives called the Chibcha grew potatoes with black flesh before the Spanish conquest in the late fifteenth century.

Potatoes are easily digested and high in fiber. They supply the body with vitamin C, several B vitamins, carbohydrates, and protein. Because they are a balanced food, potatoes became a main food source for many people. However, depending on a single food can lead to disaster.

The Irish Potato Famine

Potatoes were introduced to Ireland in the late sixteenth century. In the early 1800s, Irish farmers grew only one or two high-yielding varieties of potatoes. The Irish people, especially poor country people, ate potatoes as their main food.

In 1845, a fungus that causes a disease called late blight was accidentally brought into Ireland. Late blight destroys the leaves and tubers of potato plants. Irish potatoes were not resistant to the blight, so for the next few years, nearly all potato plants rotted in the fields. By the time the blight was over, more than one million people in Ireland had died of starvation or famine-related disease. A further one and a half million Irish people left their native country for the United States.

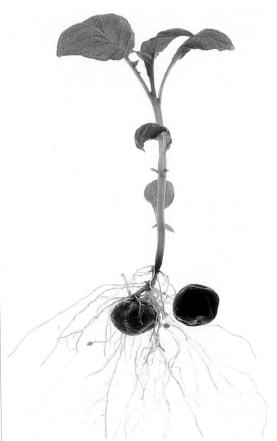

◄ *The fleshy growths called tubers on the roots of potato plants are the only part that can be eaten.*

KEY FACTS

● **Name**
Potato
(*Solanum tuberosum*)

● **Range**
Wide distribution, including northern United States, Canada, Europe, highlands of South America, New Zealand, Russia

● **Habitat**
Cool, temperate regions; now also in tropical regions

● **Appearance**
Plant up to 3½ ft (1m) tall. Leaves with oval, pointed leaflets; 1-in (3-cm) long 5-petaled flowers may be white, yellow, or purple; edible tubers growing on roots underground, with skin and flesh from white to purple; weigh a few ounces up to 4 lb (2 kg)

● **Life cycle**
Perennial

● **Uses**
Important staple food

● **Status**
Widely cultivated

See also **Deadly nightshade**

Prairie chicken

When the first settlers traveled across the great plains or prairies of central and western North America, they found a bird that they had not seen in the farmlands or open ground of Europe. They named it the prairie chicken. It was a strange-looking bird with brown and white stripes across its body. In the mating season the male has a tall crest on its head that seems to match its upright tail. However, the plains Indians had known the prairie chicken for years. Its fine feathers and breeding display inspired them to decorate their heads with feathers and perform their well-known foot-stamping dance.

There are only two species of prairie chicken in the world, the Lesser and the Greater, both of which are only found in North America.

▲ *During the winter months, in the colder part of its range, the prairie chicken keeps warm by fluffing up its feathers to trap pockets of air. This makes it look round and fat, with a very small head. This is a male Greater prairie chicken, with flashes of orange around its eyes and throat.*

Feeding habits

Prairie chickens are ground-dwelling birds, relying on tall grasses and their coloring for cover. Their diet varies according to the time of year. In the summer they eat mainly insects, especially grasshoppers. For the rest of year they eat mainly plant food: fruit, leaves, flowers, shoots, and seeds – whatever is most plentiful.

Male gathering

During the breeding season, prairie chickens gather together in groups. The males join together in a cluster organized according to seniority and share a display area that is known as a lek. There is one bird that is "senior" to the others: the dominant male. The leks of Greater prairie chickens are sometimes known as booming grounds, and those of Lesser prairie chickens are called gobbling grounds. These names reflect the activities of the males when they are trying to attract mates. The males have bare

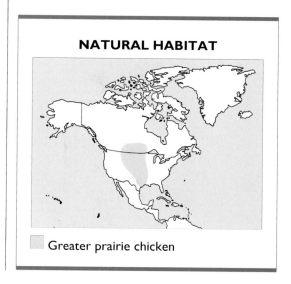

NATURAL HABITAT

Greater prairie chicken

● **Name**
Greater prairie
chicken
(*Tympanuchus cupido*)

● **Range**
Prairies of southern
Canada to Texas

● **Habitat**
Tall-grass prairie

● **Appearance**
16½-18 in (42-46 cm)
long; a brown,
chicken-like bird;
dark brown and buff,
with bars on the
upperparts and
heavily barred below;
a short, rounded tail,
black in the male,
barred in the female;
a brownish head with
a slight crest;
feathers on the feet
down to the toes

● **Food**
Insects and plants

● **Breeding**
Nest in pastures and
wood clearings; the
nest is a slight hollow
in the ground lined
with grasses; females
lay eggs during April-
June, 7-17, usually
10-12; the eggs are
incubated by the
female for 23-24
days; the chicks leave
the nest hours after
hatching

● **Status**
Endangered

yellowish-orange sacs on the sides of their throats called tympani (drums). When they form groups to court females they blow up these sacs, which attracts the females. At the same time, they rearrange their feathers, so that they have drooping wings and upright tails and crests. They call out, making a gobbling noise.

The hens that visit the lek are very choosy and usually mate with the central and most dominant male. The nest is a hollow scraped in the ground, usually lined with grasses. The Lesser prairie chicken lives in drier habitats than the Greater. Here the grass is shorter, and the birds cannot afford to grow so large. They do not grow to more than 16 in (40 cm). Because the ground is drier, they scrape a hollow in the sand for their nest.

The females of both species lay a large number of eggs, usually 10-12. This is because the ground-living young are very vulnerable to predators such as birds of prey; the greater the number of chicks that hatch, the greater the chances of some of them surviving to adulthood.

Scarce species

The numbers of both species of prairie chicken are falling, and the problem is now very serious indeed. The use of land for agriculture is the main cause of the decline in their numbers. One subspecies, called Attwater's greater prairie chicken, is endangered.

▼ *When it puts on a display, the male Greater prairie chicken takes on quite a different look. Its crest and tail feathers are erect, its wings are drooping and it has puffed up the orange "drums" on either side of its throat. It makes a loud booming noise to attract hen birds in the area.*

Prairie dog

Prairie dogs are well known for their remarkable underground communities or "towns" that at one time used to stretch over hundreds of miles. Like chipmunks and marmots, they are close relatives of the squirrels; in fact prairie dogs are a type of ground squirrel. The common name "dog" comes from the fact that these rodents communicate with one another by making a barking sound.

Prairie dogs live in scattered pockets on prairies, plains, and alpine meadows from the Canadian-United States border in central North America as far south as northern Mexico, and from Utah and Arizona across to Kansas and Oklahoma.

Hundreds of family units

Prairie dog towns consist of numerous underground burrows that stretch beneath the surface of the earth for miles and miles. Hundreds, sometimes thousands, of individuals inhabit these burrows, all of them organized into a complex social structure. The communities are divided into smaller units called wards and the wards into even smaller units called coteries. A coterie usually consists of one male, two to three adult females, and a number of young.

A family's burrow has many entrances, each one of which opens into a tunnel that leads steeply down into the earth, sometimes to depths of 9-12 ft (2.7-3.6 m). Entrance tunnels join up with other tunnels that lie parallel to the surface of the ground and lead to nesting chambers. The entrance hole may lie as much as 6 ft (1.8 m) away from the nesting chambers.

Daily life

The prairie dog spends much of its time feeding and keeping a lookout for predators as well as making certain its burrow is in good repair. It lives on a diet of grasses and herbs and eats these where it finds them; unlike many other rodents it does not store food. During cold spells in the winter months, most species of prairie dog will remain in their burrows for long periods, sleeping but not fully hibernating.

Prairie dogs are relatively easy prey for a number of predators, including coyotes, Black-footed ferrets, and some birds of

◄ This mother is teaching her pup new skills as they play outside their burrow.

KEY FACTS

- **Name**
  Black-tailed prairie dog (*Cynomys ludovicianus*)

- **Range**
  Central North America down to northern Mexico

- **Habitat**
  Short-grass prairies

- **Appearance**
  A large ground squirrel, measuring 9-14 in (23-35.5 cm), with a black-tipped tail of 2-4 in (4-11cm); a pale yellowish-brown coat with white underparts

- **Food**
  Grasses, plants; occasionally insects

- **Breeding**
  Females give birth to a single litter of 4-5 young, which are weaned at about 7 weeks

- **Status**
  Widespread, but declining in numbers

prey. When the rodent spots such an enemy, it gives a yapping alarm call to warn the others, which flee into their burrows as quickly as possible. Most prairie dogs that are caught by predators are the very young, the sick, and the old.

Underground, prairie dogs sometimes have to share their burrows with rattlesnakes, which crawl down into the tunnels to hibernate in the winter or to escape the worst of the sun's heat in the summer. When a rattlesnake is present in a nesting chamber, the prairie dog usually leaves it well alone and extends its burrow in another direction, away from the unwelcome visitor. The burrowing owl, another animal of the prairies, will sometimes take over deserted prairie dog homes for nesting.

Young prairie dogs

Most rodents are renowned for producing a large number of young every year, but prairie dogs mate only once a year in the early spring. The female gives birth about 30 days after mating and bears three to six pups at any time between March and May. The pups' eyes remain closed for about 33 days, and they are weaned in seven weeks. The adult male pushes the young males out of the burrow soon after this and they make off to dig burrows of their own. Sometimes one or two of the adult females will leave as well, making way for their daughters who may mate with their father the following year.

The prairie dog community extends into "suburbs" in this way, and this explains how the towns can spread, sometimes over vast areas. An account made in 1901

gives details of a prairie dog community that actually spread over 2400 sq miles (6216 km^2) and contained an estimated 400 million individuals!

Competition for land

Soon after the arrival of European settlers on the prairies and plains, prairie dog numbers began to decline wherever the settlers established ranches and farms. Domestic cattle and horses competed with the prairie dog for food, and the many prairie dog holes in the earth were hazards in which domestic animals twisted their feet and broke their legs. Their owners set about disposing of the prairie dogs with poison on such a large scale that at least one species, the Utah prairie dog, is now threatened.

▲ *Around the burrow entrance the prairie dog piles up loose soil and then compacts it to form walls 12-24 in (30-60 cm) high. This looks like the cone of a volcano and may be up to 6 ft (1.8 m) across. Its main purpose is to stop the burrow from flooding when it rains heavily.*

NATURAL HABITAT

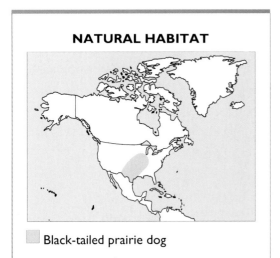

Black-tailed prairie dog

See also **Black-footed ferret**

Praying mantis

Praying mantises get their name because of the way they hold their powerful grasping arms. They have a ruthless reputation and have evolved into near perfect predators. Many people think that the female always eats the male before, during or after mating, but research has shown that the male's fate is not sealed by mating.

Perfect insect predator

Praying mantises have highly moveable heads allowing them to look in all directions without moving their bodies.

▲ *The eggs emerge from the tip of the abdomen of the female praying mantis. They are coated in a white foamy liquid that quickly hardens, protecting the eggs.*

This is very useful as it reduces the chances of them being seen by any predators. It also lessens the chances of their lunch spotting them. All praying mantises have large, complex eyes set on the top of a triangular-shaped head. They have excellent eyesight, hunting for their food during the day. Unlike insects with poor eyesight, praying mantises do not need long antennae and most species have short, thread-like ones.

Grasping arms

Praying mantises no longer use their front pair of legs for walking. Instead these legs have become more arm-like and are used for grabbing and holding their prey, while their sharp and powerful jaws cut it up into bite-sized pieces. To help them grip, the inside edges of these grasping "arms" are lined with sharp spines. The spines dig into the prey to hold it in place. To stop their lunch running away, praying mantises also have a flexible joint at their waists so they can lift their prey clear of the ground.

Most species of praying mantis have a pair of wings and a pair of wing covers. However, very few species can fly well, and in those that can it is usually the males that fly. Some of the smaller species of praying mantis have lost their wings altogether.

Keeping still is one way to avoid predators, but being hunters, praying mantises cannot wait for their food to come to them. To avoid being seen, they have evolved some amazing forms of camouflage. Many species are green and generally leaf-like, while others mimic (copy) dead leaves, twigs, moss, and even stones. Some species pretend to be flowers. Not only is this very effective camouflage, but it also attracts insects that feed on flowers, and these praying mantises feed on them.

Praying mantises are found in tropical and subtropical countries. A few small species can be found in cooler countries. They are most plentiful in forests, in both numbers of species and individuals. However, many species have evolved in other habitats such as deserts and plains.

Praying mantises are voracious feeders and will tackle prey several times larger than themselves. Indeed, they are one of the few insects to feed upon vertebrates. Some large species eat frogs, lizards, and small birds. One large species called the Chinese praying mantis, *Tenodera aridifolia*, which was introduced into North America from Asia, is recorded as having caught and eaten an adult White-footed mouse. But usually insects make up the bulk of their diet.

Mating mantises

Female praying mantises are notorious for biting the heads off their would-be mates. Although this does occasionally happen, it is usually because the female is too hungry to mate. Sometimes the male is too pushy or just clumsy. If the male's head is bitten off, he has a back-up brain that makes sure he finishes mating before he dies. Most males, however, live to mate again.

The eggs of praying mantises are not laid individually. They are laid in batches of up to 400. To make sure they stand a good chance of hatching, the female creates a foamy liquid around them that hardens after contact with the air. This structure is called an ootheca. It prevents the eggs from drying out too quickly and deters some parasitic insects. Many oothecas fall victim to parasites, however, and instead of baby praying mantises hatching, hundreds of minute adult wasps emerge – having eaten all the eggs inside.

Those oothecas that are not taken over by parasites hatch after three to eighteen weeks, depending on the species and temperature. Praying mantises from countries that have cold winters use this egg stage as a resting period when there is no food around.

▲ *This species of praying mantis from Trinidad looks like a dead leaf lying on the ground.*

KEY FACTS

● **Name**
Praying mantises (*Mantodea* order); over 1900 species including the Chinese praying mantis (*Tenodera aridifolia*)

● **Range**
Worldwide, but most numerous in the tropics and subtropics

● **Habitat**
Most habitats from forests to plains

● **Appearance**
Medium to large insects, $\frac{1}{2}$ in to 6 in (1.5 cm to 16 cm) long; highly variable in shape and color; the head is triangular in shape, sometimes with a crest; the first pair of legs is used for grasping prey; small antennae

● **Food**
Large species eat frogs, lizards, birds, and small mammals; most species eat insects

● **Breeding**
Eggs are protected by foam; they hatch into nymphs; some species actively protect their young

● **Status**
Many tropical forest species are becoming rare

Proboscis monkey

The Proboscis monkey is one of the strangest-looking primates in the world. As its name suggests, its best known feature is the large, drooping proboscis or nose of the adult male (proboscis means "trunk" in Greek). This nose may measure up to 4 in (10 cm) long and hang down over the monkey's mouth – this can cause problems when feeding, and the animal often has to move it to one side as it eats.

▲ *Here we can see clearly the large, drooping nose of this adult male Proboscis monkey. Some scientists think that this may make his voice boom louder, making him more attractive to females.*

Living in the swamps

Proboscis monkeys are large primates that are closely related to colobus monkeys. Males are almost twice the size of females and may measure up to 30 in (76 cm) long from head to rump, with a tail of about the same length and a weight of 22-50 lb (10-23 kg).

Proboscis monkeys, who are diurnal (active during the day), live in the mangrove swamps of Borneo and spend most of their time in trees. There they are extremely nimble and can move quickly through the branches. They are also good swimmers and often descend to the swamps below. The Proboscis monkey's main source of food is leaves, although they also eat flowers, fruit, and water plants. They get most of their water from their food, but they sometimes lick dew from leaves and drink rainwater from little pools where it collects in tree hollows.

Life in a troop

Proboscis monkeys are very sociable animals that gather together in large groups called troops. These may number anything from 10 to 60 individuals, and each troop has a home range of about 320 acres (1.25 km²).

The monkeys spend most of the day eating, although there are two periods of intense feeding – one in the morning and a second in the late afternoon. The whole troop feeds in the same tree at the same time, each individual sitting alone on its own branch to eat.

Once female Proboscis monkeys reach the age of four and males four or five, they are old enough to mate. There is no particular breeding season, but most births are timed so that the young are weaned when there is most nutritious food available in the trees. Unlike many mammals, it is the female Proboscis monkey who approaches the male when she is ready to mate. When she has chosen a suitable partner to target she purses her lips at him and then shakes her head from side to side. If the male is interested, he makes a pouting face back at her and they approach one another.

About 5½ months after mating, a single young is born. This baby weighs about 14 oz (0.4 kg) and measures around 8 in (20 cm) from head to rump. It is fairly well developed at birth: it can see, and its arms are strong enough for it to support its own weight as it clings to its mother's chest. It is covered in soft, downy fur and has a bright blue face that fades after a few months. In related species that have

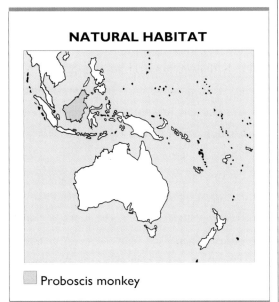

NATURAL HABITAT

Proboscis monkey

been studied closely the mother allows other females to carry her offspring, and even to suckle them.

In danger

Proboscis monkeys were once found in large numbers throughout Borneo, but hunting and the destruction of some of their favorite mangrove habitat have caused these monkeys to disappear from many lowland and coastal areas. Despite being protected in Indonesia since 1931, the Proboscis monkey is now considered an endangered species.

◄ *Proboscis monkeys spend most of their time in trees and feed mainly on leaves. The monkey has to have a complicated digestive system to cope with this kind of diet.*

KEY FACTS

● **Name**
Proboscis monkey
(*Nasalis larvatus*)

● **Range**
Borneo

● **Habitat**
Mangrove swamps

● **Appearance**
A large monkey, up to 30 in (76 cm) with a long tail; the fur is grayish-yellow to reddish-brown in color; adult males have large, drooping noses up to 4 in (10 cm) long

● **Food**
Mainly leaves and shoots; occasionally flowers and fruit

● **Breeding**
Females give birth to a single offspring, which can see at birth; it has a blue face and is covered in soft, downy fur

● **Status**
Endangered

See also **Colobus monkey**

Ptarmigan

Ptarmigans are chubby looking birds that are closely related to prairie chickens and grouse. They are members of a larger group of birds, the pheasant family.

There are three species of Ptarmigan in the world, all of which are found in North America. They are ground-dwelling birds that live on the open tundra (land that is covered by snow for much of the year) and the rocky and barren slopes and tops of high mountains.

Climatic changes

The cold climate influences the lifestyle of ptarmigans in several ways. Like most ground-dwelling birds, they have to be well camouflaged. Because their surroundings change so dramatically from summer to winter, they have two completely different sets of feathers. In the winter they are white, while in the summer they have dappled brown plumage. Their legs are well covered in feathers, and they have sharp claws to give them a good grip on icy slopes during the frozen winter months.

▲ *In her summer plumage, the female Willow ptarmigan is well disguised against the grass and scrub. She is sheltering young chicks that are equally well camouflaged. They grow rapidly on a rich diet of caterpillars and other insects, as well as spiders. The parents continue to tend them until they are at least two months old.*

Ptarmigans' diet also varies with the seasons. In the summer the trees and shrubs provide a good food supply. They eat the tender leaves and flower buds of willows, birches, and alders, and the fruit of blueberries, cranberries, crowberries, and kinnikinnick (the plants used to make up the "tobacco" mixture of the American Indians and pioneers in Ohio). They also pick up and eat insects. During the winter, food is much more sparse. Ptarmigans search out twigs and buds of willow, buds and catkins of dwarf birches, and plant material from other trees and bushes.

At night, particularly in the winter, ptarmigans roost close together; sometimes several dozen share a site. They sleep on the ground, but although they spend much of the day walking, they always fly to

NATURAL HABITAT

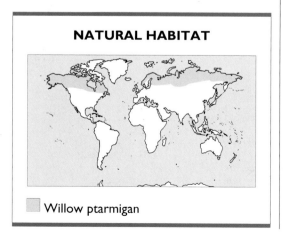

□ Willow ptarmigan

their roosting sites that are buried in the snow. There is a simple reason for this: if they were to walk through the snow to their "bedrooms," predators such as foxes and lynx would find them easily. By flying straight into the snowdrifts they leave no telltale footprints.

Family life

When the spring arrives in the northern wastelands where these birds live, the mating season begins. As the snow recedes, fresh vegetation sprouts, providing food for the young. The males select a bare patch of ground to perform their display: they strut up and down with their feathers puffed up. If other males approach, there may be fierce battles. They have been known to pull each other's feathers out and draw blood. While the

▼ *Like many animals that live in the Arctic circle, the ptarmigan has white winter coloring. It feeds on seeds and buds peeping through the snow.*

males battle it out, the females lurk in the undergrowth. The victor gains the right to mate with the female, attracting her with his strutting display. After mating, the females scrape a hollow in the ground and lay their eggs. There are usually six eggs, although 17 have been recorded in a nest.

While the female keeps the eggs warm the male remains with her, helping to defend her and her clutch. The male molts later than the female, so he still has his conspicuous white winter feathers. This helps to distract the attention of predators away from the well-camouflaged female. The male is surprisingly aggressive, and has been seen flying at large gulls and even Grizzly bears.

Because they live in remote areas, ptarmigans have not suffered from the invasion of humans. The coniferous forests have not been exploited in the same way as grasslands and rainforests further south.

The Willow ptarmigan, the largest of the three species, is the state bird of Alaska.

KEY FACTS

● **Name**
Willow ptarmigan
(*Lagopus lagopus*)

● **Range**
Northern part of the northern hemisphere, from Alaska, across Canada to Newfoundland, and through Eurasia

● **Habitat**
Summer: open tundra and the upper edge of timberline; winter: sheltered valleys

● **Appearance**
15-17 in (38-43 cm) long; the plumage is mainly brown in the summer and white in the winter

● **Food**
Fruit, buds, leaves, and shoots; also insects

● **Breeding**
The nest is a hollow in the ground, lined with grasses and feathers; usually 6-7 eggs incubated by the female for 21-22 days; the male defends the female; the young leave the nest soon after hatching; parental care for 2 months

● **Status**
Common in the Arctic, but numbers vary greatly

See also **Grouse, Mountain, Tundra**

735

Puffer fish

KEY FACTS

• **Name**
Spotted puffer fish
(*Arothron meleagris*)

• **Range**
Western and central
Pacific Ocean,
including Hawaiian
Islands

• **Habitat**
Shallow coastal
waters; coral reefs
and tidal lagoons

• **Appearance**
12 in (30 cm) long;
a stocky, flattened
body that is dark
brown and covered
in white spots;
rounded fins; eyes
protrude from the
top of the head

• **Food**
Plant and animal
material, including
small fish and
crustaceans

• **Breeding**
Female lays eggs
that are attached to
plants; there may be
some parental care
of the eggs, but the
young fish have to
fend for themselves

• **Status**
Widespread but rare
in some parts of its
range

The common name "puffer fish" is given to a large number of fish belonging to a family of over 100 species that is technically called the *Tetraodontidae*. These fish also have a large number of other common names including swellfish, toadfish (Australia), tobies (South Africa), blowfish (North America), and fugu (Japan). Most are saltwater fish, but a few species have made their way up rivers and live in freshwater habitats.

The ability to blow themselves up into a ball is the most remarkable feature linking all the different kinds of puffer fish. This is also the reason for their common name.

On the defensive

All the puffer fish are rather plump, stout-bodied, rounded fish. They have small and

▲ *Puffer fish (this is a Spotted puffer fish) have strange-looking beaks that they use to crack open the shells of seafood to eat the soft insides.*

rounded fins that they use as paddles, so they are not very efficient swimmers. However, they have a large number of ways of defending themselves against their predators – the larger fish and sea mammals that share their tropical home.

First, most species have spotted or mottled skins that help to disguise them against the rocks and seaweed. If the fish become frightened or agitated, they then use a most unusual form of defense – they puff themselves up by taking gulps of water or air to fill their stomachs. This makes the spines on their bodies, which normally lie flat against their skin, stand erect. Some species only puff themselves up a little, while others can blow up like a balloon until they are totally spherical. Puffed-up puffer fish cannot swim at all because their fins are buried in their bodies. They usually float to the surface and drift until the danger has passed. Then they deflate themselves by letting the air out of their stomachs. Sometimes they get washed ashore while they are puffed up.

As a third form of defense some puffer fish have eye-like patterns that show around their tails. This is a pattern that is repeatedly found in fish and insects; the idea is that larger-than-life eyes should scare away all but the most intrepid predators. Puffer fish have yet another method of defense: their sexual organs and parts of their intestines are highly poisonous. Usually predators soon learn which fish are poisonous and avoid them. However, in spite of all its defenses, puffer fish are regularly eaten by larger neighbors.

Tasty but dangerous

In Japan, puffer fish have been regarded as a delicacy for thousands of years. But the toxins (poisons) they carry to deter underwater predators and birds are also

toxic to humans. The Japanese have specially trained chefs who remove the poisonous parts of the fish and serve them in special restaurants. However, even though the chefs have years of training, some people die every year from eating this delicacy.

Feeding and breeding

Most puffer fish live in relatively shallow water close to the shore line. They are particularly common around coral reefs. Here they live on slow-moving, hard-shelled animals such as mollusks and crustaceans. They find their prey by shooting a stream of water from their mouths at the sandy seabed to clear away the debris and expose their food supply.

Little is known about how puffer fish breed, but they are thought to attach their eggs to plants while they develop. Some males have been observed guarding the eggs and fanning water over them to keep them clean and free from algae or parasites. The eggs are highly poisonous, which helps to deter predators.

▲ *Once it is puffed up, no fish could get its jaws around the spiny ball that the puffer fish turns itself into. Another family of fish, with the same habit of blowing themselves up into balls, is the Diodontidae, known as the porcupine fish or burrfish.*

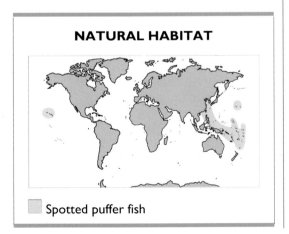

NATURAL HABITAT

Spotted puffer fish

737

Puffin

There are three species of puffin, all found in North America. The Atlantic or Common puffin is the best known, found in northeast North America and in Europe. On the west coast, there are two species, the Horned puffin and the Tufted puffin. The Horned puffin breeds in Siberia, moving south to California and to Japan in winter. The Tufted puffin is found in northeast Asia, the Aleutians, and down the west coast of North America.

Sea lovers

Puffins are sea-loving birds, spending most of their lives at sea, either flying above the water, sitting on the surface like a duck, or diving below in search of food. Their diet consists of a wide range of fish and marine invertebrates. They dive, either from the air or from swimming on the surface of the water, and can swim very fast beneath the surface using their wings to "fly" through the water. Their feet are spaced well apart and act as rudders. They have dense, waterproof feathers that cannot become waterlogged.

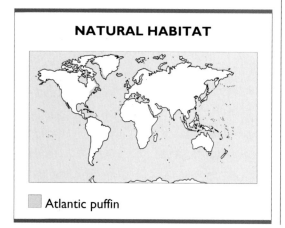

NATURAL HABITAT

Atlantic puffin

Most of the year the puffin swallows its prey under water, but during the breeding season adult puffins can be seen with rows of fish in their mouths. They hold them crosswise, and they look quite comical with the sleek, silver fish drooping like a mustache on either side of the bill. They are often bullied by gulls and skuas when they have their mouths full of food for their young. The gulls do not usually harm the adults, but they chase and harrass them until they give up their catch.

The family burrow

The breeding season starts in the spring. The birds move to the northern part of their range, seeking out cliffs and deserted rocky outcrops. They often come back to the same breeding sites year after year. At the start of the breeding season, the adults develop their characteristic, colorful bills. They have orange-red tips, a blue band, and a border of yellow at the base of the

▲ *Puffins have special spines on their tongues and the top part of their bills so that they can grip as many as 50 tiny fish at a time. The young chicks eat their own weight in fish every day.*

▶ *Puffins are often described as the clowns of the bird world. The features that earn them this name include their bright beaks, their sad-looking eyes set into a white face, their clumsy looking flight, and their waddling walk.*

bill. Part of the mating ritual involves "billing" – rattling their bills together. The birds gather together in a large flock, floating on the surface of the water. The same pair usually mate together each year, although they go their separate ways during the winter months.

At the start of the breeding season, the pair check out the nest burrow they have used in previous years. They clean it and line it with grass, seaweed, and feathers. If the pair do not already have a burrow, the male digs one out using his bill as an axe and shoveling out the soil with his claws and webbed feet.

The female lays a single egg and the adults share the task of keeping the egg warm until it is ready to hatch – 42 days after laying. Puffins do not have the energy to raise more than one chick each year because the burrow is a long way from the birds' fishing grounds and the chicks have big appetites.

The young puffins are very vulnerable when they come out of their burrows.

The parents leave them to make their first flight from their clifftop burrow at night, when there are no gulls or larger birds around to attack them. (The White-tailed fish eagle has been seen catching and eating young puffins in flight.)

Protection from humans

Puffins have suffered greatly from human intervention. They are meaty birds, and have been popular as food for hundreds of years. In some countries, hunters used to attract them by putting out stuffed puffins so the new arrivals would come to join the "colony" and the hunters could catch them with nets.

The introduction of small mammals to the islands that are the puffins' breeding grounds has also reduced their numbers. They are susceptible to feather damage from oil spillage, and they have to work hard to find enough food now that so many parts of the North Atlantic and North Pacific are plundered by the fishing industry. Puffins are protected by law.

KEY FACTS

● **Name**
Atlantic or Common puffin (*Fratercula arctica*)

● **Range**
Breeds along rocky coasts of the North Atlantic from Maine to Greenland, and in northern Europe

● **Habitat**
Coastal cliffs; winters at sea

● **Appearance**
$11\frac{1}{2}$-$13\frac{1}{2}$ in (29-34 cm) tall; short, stocky body; black upperparts; white cheeks and breast; a large triangular bill, bright reddish-orange with a blue band edged in yellow; after the breeding season the outer layers of the bill are shed; both sexes look similar

● **Food**
Small fishes, mollusks, and crustaceans

● **Breeding**
Gather in colonies and nest in burrows 2-4 ft (60-120 cm) deep; a single egg is incubated by both parents for about 42 days

● **Status**
Common in limited areas

See also **Gull, Skua**

Puma

Also known as the cougar or Mountain lion, the puma is a muscular, powerful cat. It is the largest of the group known as the small cats (which includes its close cousins the ocelot, bobcat, and lynx), growing up to 75 in (195 cm) and weighing up to 225 lb (100 kg).

A mighty hunter

The puma is a carnivore (meat eater) and an efficient hunter. It will hunt almost anything that moves, from small rodents to large mammals such as deer. It is a solitary animal and prefers to hunt alone by stealth, creeping up on its prey silently until it is close enough to pounce. It is diurnal (active during the day), although most of its hunting is done when the light

NATURAL HABITAT

Puma

▲ *Also known as the Mountain lion, the puma often inhabits rocky, mountainous country. It is found from southern Canada, down through the western U.S., Central America, and South America as far as Patagonia.*

is fading, at dawn or dusk. Then its brownish-gray coat allows this cunning cat to melt into the shadows and become almost invisible to its unsuspecting victims.

If necessary, the puma sprints after its prey, leaping onto the animal's back with a single bound that may cover up to 23 ft (7 m). Then it wrestles its victim to the ground, killing it with a fatal bite to the back of the neck and dragging the carcass across the ground with its powerful paws.

Sometimes the puma may follow animals such as raccoons into the trees. It is an excellent climber and can jump nimbly from the branches to the ground – up to 65 ft (20 m) below!

Following the migrating prey

Both sexes live alone and have their own territories; those of female pumas are usually much smaller than those of males and may overlap in several places. These home ranges vary in size, depending on the season and the availability of prey.

During the summer when prey is plentiful, male home ranges may extend up to 110 sq miles (290 km^2). However, in the winter they decrease to about 50 sq miles (130 km^2) and the whole territory may even move southward, following the seasonal migration of the puma's favorite prey, the elk and Mule deer. Despite their territorial nature, pumas tend to avoid each other as much as possible and do not often fight to defend their home ranges.

During the mating season, which may be at any time of year but is often in the winter months, a male puma travels throughout his range looking for a female whose territory overlaps his. By sniffing scent markings and tracks, he can detect if a particular female is ready to mate. Once he has found a suitable partner, he stays by her side for two weeks until she allows him to mate with her, and then he leaves.

About three months after mating, the female finds a comfortable den in thick vegetation or a cave and gives birth to a litter of three or four cubs. These are blind and helpless, and their coats are covered in large spots that fade by the time they are six months old. The mother raises them alone without the father, suckling them for three months and bringing them small pieces of meat from the age of six weeks onward. She teaches them how to hunt and survive until they are about two years old, when they leave her to establish their own home ranges.

▼ *The puma is an efficient hunting cat, with huge, powerful paws and claws that can rip flesh. This puma is sharpening his claws on a log.*

KEY FACTS

● **Name**
Puma, cougar, or Mountain lion
(*Felis concolor*)

● **Range**
Southern Canada, the western U.S., Florida, Central America, western South America

● **Habitat**
Rocky terrain; forests, including conifer, deciduous, and tropical; grasslands; deserts

● **Appearance**
40-75 in (105-195 cm) from head to rump, with a tail of 25-30 in (67-78 cm); a plain coat, tawny or gray-brown to black in color; cubs are spotted until they are about 6 months old

● **Food**
Most animals, from small rodents to deer as large as elk; occasionally domestic livestock; sometimes insects and grass

● **Breeding**
Females give birth to a litter of 2-6 cubs (usually 3 or 4) that are weaned at about 3 months old

● **Status**
Threatened in some parts of its range

Python

◄ *This Reticulated python uses its tongue to "sniff." It draws chemicals in the air to a very sensitive organ in its mouth.*

Members of the python family are among the largest snakes in the world. They are famous for their ability to squeeze their prey to death – and then swallow it whole! Their coloring ranges from a uniform brown or green to regular, bold patterns with diamond-shaped blotches.

Shapes and sizes

Most of the 27 species of python are found in the rainforests and grasslands of Africa, Asia, and Australasia. Some scientists include the Mexican burrowing python (*Loxocemus bicolor*) in the same family as the rest of the pythons. It is the only python found in America.

Most species are about 10-20 ft (3-6 m) long. The smallest is the West Australian dwarf python, which only grows to 20 in (50 cm) and the largest is the Reticulated python, which grows up to 33 ft (10 m) long. Although the Reticulated python is enormous, it is welcomed in many parts of the world because it feeds on small pests such as rats.

However, pythons are skilled feeders and do not restrict their diet to farm and household pests. For example, the African rock python (*Python sebae*) eats wild pigs and small antelopes. The Indian python (*P. molurus*) tackles animals as large as leopards. Some of the larger species of python have been known to kill and eat humans (although usually only young or weak people have been harmed).

Most pythons come out at night, and as they have poor eyesight, they must detect their prey by scent (using their tongues) and heat. They have heat-sensitive pits in their upper lips that detect animals such

KEY FACTS

● **Name**
Reticulated python
(*Python reticulatus*)

● **Range**
Southeast Asia and Indonesia

● **Habitat**
Forests

● **Appearance**
Largest of the pythons, up to 33 ft (10 m) long; its intricate pattern camouflages it well in areas of light and shade

● **Food**
Mammals

● **Breeding**
Female lays up to 100 eggs; the newly hatched young are 24-30 in (60-75 cm) long; they grow at a rate of about 24 in (60 cm) per year for the first few years

● **Status**
Widespread

as birds and rats, which are warmer than their surroundings.

These special adaptations mean that they can locate their prey in total darkness. Once they have caught their prey, they have several other special features that help them to consume it. Their jaws have backward-pointing teeth that, although they are not venom-producing, will hold the prey firmly. They seize their prey with their mouths and then swiftly coil themselves around it and kill it by tightening the coils so that the victim cannot expand its chest to breathe. In fact, the victim dies by suffocation rather than by crushing.

Satisfied snakes

Once the prey is dead, the python swallows it whole. It opens its mouth wide, and its special jaws dislocate if the creature it is eating is large. It may take several hours for the snake to swallow its prey. After feeding on large animals they become grotesquely fat and find it very difficult to move. Indeed they may go may

▲ Female pythons such as this Green tree python guard their eggs by coiling around them. In cooler zones this helps to keep the temperature of the eggs constant at around 85°F (30°C).

go for weeks without eating again.

Pythons lay large numbers of eggs and are unusual for snakes in that they spend time caring for the eggs. In the case of the Reticulated python, there may be as many as 100 to look after.

Threats to pythons

Pythons have been persecuted for their feeding habits and killed for their skins, which were popular for shoes and fashion accessories. Their numbers are also falling due to the destruction of their habitat.

NATURAL HABITAT

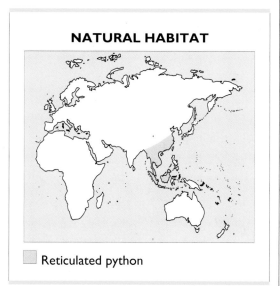

▨ Reticulated python

See also **Anaconda**

743

Quail

Quails are round-bodied game birds that are very closely related to pheasants and grouse (including prairie chickens and ptarmigans). They are often referred to as wood partridges because they generally prefer living in forests and woodlands to the open plains, although this does depend on the species. The New World quails are restricted to North, Central, and South America. There are 28 species in all, of which six species are native to North America. There are 11 species of Old World quail, found in Africa, Asia, and Australia; the Common quail is a summer visitor to Europe, migrating to Africa in the winter.

Ground dwellers

Quails are small birds, seldom more than 12 in (30 cm) long. Although their colors are fairly muted in beige, brown, black, and white, some species are quite boldly marked with black, white, buff, and gray stripes or mottling. Their stout bills are ideal for pecking at seeds, grains, and fruit, and are also used to catch insects occasionally. They have long, strong legs

NATURAL HABITAT

Northern bobwhite quail

▲ *The Scaled quail of the southwestern states takes its name from the pattern of the feathers on its breast, which look like the scales of a fish. It is one of the species of quail that has a crest.*

▶ *Quails are ground-living birds, spending their time pecking around the undergrowth and grasslands where they live. Here is a male Northern bobwhite with two females or younger birds.*

with four toes and sharp claws, which they use to scratch the ground for food.

Quails feed for a couple of hours after sunrise and a couple more hours before sunset, resting in the middle of the day.

Bobbing and calling

The best known quails in North America are probably the bobwhites or Northern bobwhites. They live in flocks known as coveys for much of the year, feeding and roosting together. At night they gather together to sleep on the ground in groups of about 10-15. Each group forms a circle with their heads pointing outward and their tails pointing to the sky. Their bodies are packed closely together to conserve body heat. If one detects danger, it instantly warns the others and they all rise with a loud roar of wings. They scatter and reassemble to feed together the next morning when danger is past.

The bobwhite gets its name from its distinctive call. In the spring, at the start of the breeding season, the male calls out from a perch to challenge other birds, and to make it clear that this is his territory and the female in the area is his partner. The call is a distinctive whistled "bob-WHITE" or "bob-bob-WHITE." Having established his rights, the male courts the female, spreading his wings and tail and bowing and turning to show white markings. Like other related species, the bobwhite lays a large number of eggs because, being ground-dwelling birds, they are very vulnerable to predators. Soon after hatching, the young are ready to follow their parents in search of food. In the late summer and early fall, the families join together in coveys of up to 30 birds.

Western cousins

There are fewer bobwhites to the west of the Rocky mountains, but the California quail is common in open habitats including coastal scrublands, woodland edges, and parks. It is the state bird of California.

See also **Grouse**

KEY FACTS

● **Name**
Northern bobwhite or Bobwhite quail
(*Colinus virginianus*)

● **Range**
Resident over almost all the eastern U.S. and Canada; intro-duced into the west

● **Habitat**
Brushlands, open woodlands, farms, dry grasslands

● **Appearance**
9½-10½ in (24-27cm) long; red-brown coloring; the male has a white stripe over the eyes and a white throat

● **Food**
Seeds, grains, wild fruit, leaves, insects

● **Breeding**
Males fight and display for the right to females; the nest is a shallow hollow in the ground, lined and arched over with grasses, with a small opening; usually 14-16 eggs are laid; the eggs are incubated for 23-24 days; the young leave the nest soon after hatching

● **Status**
Common; a subspecies, the Masked bobwhite is endangered

Quetzal

The quetzal is part of the trogon family, a small family of birds found in the tropical rainforests across the world, from Central and South America and Africa to Southeast Asia. The Resplendent quetzal, like so many birds of these regions, has brilliant plumage, the male glowing from head to foot. There are five species of quetzal, all of which are restricted to Central and South America.

The marvelous coloring of quetzals has impressed humans for thousands of years. Aztecs and Mayans worshipped it as a god of the air, and the long feathers that trail from the male's tail were plucked (without harming the birds) for use in ancient ceremonies. In Guatemala the quetzal is the national bird, the currency is named after it, and it is regarded as a symbol of freedom. Indeed, Guatemalans maintain that if a quetzal is kept in captivity it soon dies of a broken heart. It is certainly true that quetzals do not survive for long in captivity.

NATURAL HABITAT

Resplendent quetzal

The male is shiny green and blue in color, with a red breast and belly. Perhaps the most remarkable part of its plumage is its trailing tail coverts. These fine feathers are not actually part of his tail, but grow from just above it, completely hiding it. There are just four of these feathers, and the two central ones may be as much as 2 ft (60 cm) long.

High fliers

Quetzals live high in the humid forests covering the mountains of Mexico and Guatemala, and in the spine of Central America as far south as western Panama. They live mainly in the high canopy of the forests, sometimes soaring above the trees

▲ *The Resplendent quetzal's beak is rather weak and its skin is very frail. Although the beak is strong enough to eat fruit and seeds in the canopy of the rainforest, these birds can only nest in rotten trees that are easy to hollow out. The male has bristly feathers on its head that form a narrow crest.*

to attract other birds. They do not come down to ground level because they find all they need in the treetops. They can pluck food from the trees without having to perch, and they have poorly developed legs, with their feet tucked in close to their bodies.

The main food of quetzals is fruit, but they also eat insects, small frogs, lizards, and snails that they find climbing in the forests. As well as being spectacular birds, they are also easily injured. Bird watchers have discovered that they have very thin skin and that their feathers fall out very easily. Perhaps this is the reason that they do not land very often.

Family ways

For most of the year, quetzals spend their time on their own, flying through the jungle picking at the plentiful food. The breeding season for the Resplendent quetzal is between February and June. The male attracts a female and performs a display, soaring high above the forest canopy and then diving back into the dense vegetation. As it flies, it gives a "wac-wac" call to attract possible mates.

After mating, both birds work together to carve out a hole in a tree trunk. Because they do not have strong bills, they have to choose a decayed tree with a rotten center that can be dug out easily. The female lays two eggs, and the parents take turns to keep them warm. When it is the male's turn, he has to be very careful with the long feathers that trail from his tail. When the male enters the nesting hole, he turns around carefully so that the trailing feathers are arched over his back.

He pokes his head out of the hole with his feathers still showing above. In some years when food is plentiful, quetzals may raise two broods in a single breeding season.

Resplendent quetzals are endangered due to the invasion of their territory and the destruction of their natural habitat.

▲ *The male Resplendent quetzal has two trailing "tail" feathers. These feathers may get damaged and broken during the breeding season, but he will grow new ones for the following year.*

KEY FACTS

- **Name**
Resplendent quetzal
(*Pharomachru mocino*)

- **Range**
Southern Mexico
to western Panama

- **Habitat**
Humid mountain
forests

- **Appearance**
14-15 in (35.5-38 cm) long; the male is green on the head, back, chest, wings, and tail coverts; a white tail with tail coverts up to 24 in (60 cm); a red belly; the female is duller green above, with a bronze head; mostly brownish-gray below; a metallic green chest and red belly

- **Food**
Fruit; also insects, frogs, lizards, snails

- **Breeding**
The nest is a deep, unlined cavity 14-90 ft (4.3-27 m) up in a decaying trunk; the eggs are laid March-June; the female incubates the eggs by night and the male by day for 17-19 days; the young are fed by both parents

- **Status**
Endangered

Quillwort

Before the dinosaurs, more than 300 million years ago, much land was covered in forest. Unlike modern forests where the trees (flowering plants and gymnosperms) bear seeds, the dominant plants were giant spore-bearing ferns, club mosses, and horsetails. Club mosses were the tallest trees, and they towered over the lush forests that were home to the earliest amphibians, reptiles, and winged insects. Over millions of years, the huge amounts of wood, leaves, and spores produced by these plants turned into coal, which is a widely used modern fuel. The closest living relatives of the now-extinct giant club mosses are small, herbaceous (leafy) plants called quillworts.

Setting the stage

Quillworts and club mosses are in the division *Lycophyta*, an early and simple group of vascular plants. A vascular plant has inner tissues specialized for carrying food and water to all plant parts. *Lycophytes* have true roots, stems, and leaves, make their own food using the sun's energy, and reproduce by spores

▲ *This overhead view of a quillwort (Isoetes histrix) shows how the leaves grow in a spiral arrangement from the corm in the center.*

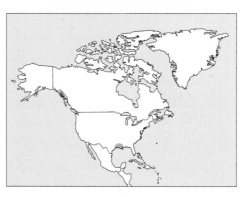

NATURAL HABITAT

▢ Louisiana quillwort

(not seeds). Many kinds lived millions of years ago, but only about 1200 species in about six genera (groups) exist today.

Quillworts (genus *Isoetes*) got their name because of the spirally arranged groups of pointy, slender, grass- or quill-like leaves that emerge from the top of a corm. A corm is a fleshy, upright, underground stem that stores food for the plant. The plant's many forked roots emerge from the bottom of the corm. Quillwort spores develop inside a round or oval capsule sunk in the leaf bases. Two

▶ *The tall, spiky leaves of this quillwort (Isoetes lacustris) look just like the quills from which the plant gets its name.*

types of spores are produced – large female spores and smaller male ones. A male spore must fertilize a female one for a new quillwort to grow.

Most of the 130 or so species of quillwort are water plants: they are aquatic. They grow in cool, swampy areas near lakes and rivers and survive long periods partially covered with water. In short, most quillworts thrive in wetlands.

A Louisiana listing

Louisiana quillwort (*Isoetes louisianensis*) is a small aquatic plant with rounded, hollow leaves 6-16 in (15-40 cm) long. Its spore capsule is notably marked with brown streaks. Louisiana quillwort grows on the sand and gravel bars of midsized creeks. During the rainy season, Louisiana quillwort is regularly covered with up to 20 in (50 cm) of water.

In 1992, the federal government listed Louisiana quillwort as an endangered species. Scientists had found small groups of this plant growing in only five locations along streams in Louisiana. Louisiana quillwort is in danger of extinction.

Why is this plant endangered?

Louisiana quillwort is very sensitive to disturbances in its freshwater habitat. Any activity that upsets the stability or character of its habitat will affect – and likely kill – the quillwort. Many of the streams where Louisiana quillwort once grew have had their banks stripped of the trees that hold the soil and shade the water's edge. When it rains, loose mud slides off the banks and clogs the stream. When loggers clear-cut, they often destroy all the plants in the area. Logging has also left stream banks hot, dry, and sun-baked, raising the near-shore water temperature, and killing the plants and animals that need cool shade. Sand and gravel mining, and the sludge and pollution that result, also ruin this habitat.

Though Louisiana quillwort is now listed as endangered, scientists are still studying its biology and the kind of habitat it needs to develop long-term plans for its proper protection. To protect this species they will most probably have to make agreements with landowners so that the quillwort's

wetland habitat can be preserved. Other related quillworts on the endangered species list include black-spored quillwort (*I. melanospora*, Georgia and South Carolina) and mat-forming quillwort (*I. tegetiformans*, Georgia).

See also **Club moss, Fern**

Rabbit

They are soft, furry, and cute. They have long ears and little twitchy noses. But the question remains ... Is the hare that raced the tortoise the same as the White Rabbit that Alice met in Wonderland?

Same but different

Both rabbits and hares are mammals belonging to the animal order *Lagomorpha*. Hares and rabbits have short front legs and longer, more powerful back legs. They have a short, furry tail. Both are plant-eaters. Their teeth grow throughout their life. They have sharp "eye" teeth for cutting plant stems and "peg" teeth for grinding plant food. Hares and rabbits

▲ *The Black-tailed jackrabbit's ears are 4-5 in (10-12 cm) long.*

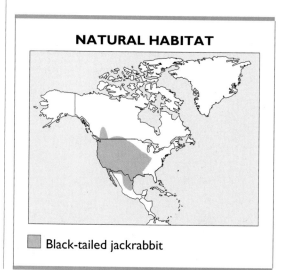

NATURAL HABITAT

☐ Black-tailed jackrabbit

sleep during the day and feed at night. Both *lagomorphs* are eaten by predators (hunting animals) such as coyotes, foxes, eagles, hawks, and owls. A lucky *lagomorph* may live to be 13 years old. Rabbits and hares usually give birth to young several times a year.

But hares and rabbits differ in some ways. Rabbits' ears are shorter than hares' ears, and their hearing is not quite as good. Rabbits depend more on their sense of smell to detect danger. Rabbits look for food near plant cover or near their nests. They hop into dense vegetation or to their nest when they sense danger. Many species of rabbit prefer living in groups, though the common Eastern cottontail prefers the solitary life. Rabbits give birth to helpless, blind, and naked young that need a lot of care from their parents.

Hares (also called jackrabbits) have long ears and very sharp hearing. Their long ears swivel to pick up the tiniest sound. If the sound means "danger," they can run to safety at speeds of up to 50 mph (80km/h). Because of their speed, hares forage in more open country farther from their homes. Hares prefer living alone. They give birth to hairy young; perhaps this is how they got their

▶ *Young rabbits need
a lot of parental care.*

name. Young hares, called leverets, are covered with fur at birth. Their open eyes can see. They can even hop around within hours after they are born. After a few weeks, the young hares leave the nest.

Black-tailed jackrabbit

The Black-tailed jackrabbit (*Lepus californicus*) is the most common hare in the western United States. It lives in different habitats but prefers the dry, short-grass regions of the Southwest and Great Plains. Black-tailed jackrabbits are generally gray with a black stripe running from the lower back to the top of its bushy tail. A typical black-tailed jackrabbit is about 22 in (53 cm) long and weighs about 6 lb (2.5 kg). Its back legs are so strong, it can bound up to 20 ft (6 m) in a single leap.

Home on the range

Most hares live in shallow hollows on the ground. The Black-tailed jackrabbit is the only hare that uses a burrow to avoid the scorching heat of the high-desert sun. The Black-tail may sleep in its burrow all day. During the cooler night, it comes out to

find food. Black-tailed jackrabbits eat plants such as grasses, sagebrush, and snakeweed. If the desert sun dries these plants out, it may eat cactus. The hare has a clever way of eating spiny cacti. First it carefully nibbles the flesh around a cactus spine. When the spine becomes loose, the hare pulls it out of the cactus. Then the jackrabbit feasts on the delicious, juicy cactus flesh beneath.

Breeding like rabbits ... almost

Rabbits are famous for the extraordinary number of young they can produce each year. Rabbits often have six or more litters of four to twelve young each during the breeding season. Young develop in their mother's body for about 28 days before they are born blind, hairless, and helpless. The hare's more developed young are produced in up to six litters of four or five young each.

Jackrabbits have complex mating behavior. The male boldly approaches a female. If she's interested in him, she will start jumping around – and he will too. Then they chase each other, zigging and zagging and hopping in the air. About 47 days after they mate, the female gives birth.

The young are born in a shallow "form" or depression in the ground. Within 24 hours after birth, the young may start exploring the world outside the form.

Raccoon

A well-loved animal in many stories and folktales, the raccoon is an intelligent and adaptable creature. Its natural habitat is broad-leaved and mixed woodlands, usually near water. However, because many woods have been cleared for timber and farmland, the raccoon has been forced to move out into more open country and has even invaded the suburbs of towns.

Like other carnivores (meat-eating animals) the raccoon has sharp claws on its feet, specialized teeth that are made for biting and tearing flesh, and highly developed senses for searching out prey. However, the raccoon is not a strict carnivore; it eats a good deal of plant material in addition to meat, a characteristic it shares with some members of the bear family.

The Common or North American raccoon is found from Canada to Central America. It is a stout, short-legged creature with a pointed muzzle. A relative, the Crab-eating raccoon, is found in South America, particularly on the east coast of the continent.

▲ Common or North American raccoons like this one feed on a wide variety of small creatures and plant material. These little carnivores (meat eaters) like to catch frogs and crayfish as well as small invertebrates such as earthworms and insects. They are often found living near water.

The masked bandit

The raccoon's long, furry, ringed tail and masked face are probably its best known features. The coat is iron gray or brownish and the tail is ringed with black markings; the black mask extends across the cheeks from the eyes. The animal has been hunted for its "coon skin" for centuries, a practice that still goes on today, although in some cases hunters are motivated by the damage raccoons do to food crops.

Raccoons spend almost as much time in trees as they do on the ground, and they are also excellent swimmers. They live alone, except for females with young, and make a home in a hollow tree or a rock crevice. In open country they sometimes seek out deserted foxholes or shelter in barns and other farmyard buildings. Where raccoons have moved into city suburbs they frequently make use of their ability to climb in order to make dens in attics. Raccoons are active at night, and it is then that they climb down from the roof to raid garbage cans for food.

KEY FACTS

● **Name**
North American or Common raccoon (*Procyon lotor*)

● **Range**
Northern Alberta through most of the U.S. to Central America

● **Habitat**
Traditionally in broad-leaved and mixed woods near water; now also found in open country and suburbs

● **Appearance**
A fairly small animal, measuring 24-36 in (60-90 cm) from head to tail and weighing 8-19 lb (3.6-8.6 kg); a gray to brownish coat, more lightly colored underneath; a black mask on the face and a black-ringed tail

● **Food**
Crayfish, frogs, insects, earthworms; fruit and farm crops such as corn

● **Breeding**
Female gives birth to a litter of 1-8 young between April and June; the young remain with their mother for 1 year

● **Status**
Common

Females and young

Raccoons mate in late winter, usually during January or February. Each female gives birth 2-2½ months later, usually to two to five young, which are born with a fuzzy coat and with their eyes closed. The mother takes great care of them and, although they are weaned at about two months and then begin to hunt for their

▲ *One of the raccoon's most remarkable features is its forepaws, which have five fingers. Like humans, raccoons can use the "hands" to manipulate objects: they have even been known to untie ropes and remove lids from jars.*

own food, they stay with her until they are about a year old.

A strange habit

For years people believed that raccoons washed their food before eating it. This stemmed from watching raccoons kept in captivity, which have a habit of putting their food into water and then taking it out again. It is thought that this practice arose because raccoons living in the wild use their forepaws in a paddling motion when looking for food in the water; when kept on land they are deprived of this method of hunting and attempt to make up for this "missed behavior."

NATURAL HABITAT

North American raccoon

See also **Suburban habitat**

Rafflesia

◄ *The Monster flower (Rafflesia arnoldii; shown left) produces the largest single flower in the world.*

KEY FACTS

● **Name**
Monster flower
(*Rafflesia arnoldii*)

● **Range**
Borneo and Sumatra

● **Habitat**
Rainforests

● **Appearance**
The only part of the plant to appear above ground is a huge cream-mottled orange, red, or purplish-brown flower, weighing up to 24 lb (11 kg) and measuring almost 3.3 ft (1 m) across; 5 fleshy "petals" surround a central cup, which contains a raised disk covered with spikes

● **Life cycle**
Perennial

● **Uses**
None known

● **Status**
Common within its range

If you were to wander through the hot, steamy forested mountains of Borneo and Sumatra, you might stumble across a massive, leathery structure, mottled cream and bright reddish orange, sitting in your path. This is the aptly named Monster flower (*Rafflesia arnoldii*), the biggest single flower in the world. It may measure up to 2.7 ft (80 cm) in diameter and weigh 15 lb (7 kg). The Monster flower belongs to a group of about 12 closely related species found in Southeast Asia.

Greedy parasites

The Monster flower was first discovered in Sumatra in 1818, by a British explorer, Sir Thomas Stamford Raffles (1781-1826), who later founded Singapore. The whole family *Rafflesiaceae* was named for him. Along with all its close relatives, the Monster flower is a parasite. This means that it lives completely on the nutrients and water from other plants. Many experts believe that this is why it is able to grow to such an enormous size: it is not restricted to providing its own energy for growth, as most plants are.

Unlike many other plant parasites, *Rafflesia* species do not attach themselves to the outside of the host plant. Instead, these plants make their home on the inside of the stem or roots, where they exist as a spreading network of cells. You would hardly know the Monster flower was there until its enormous single flower shows itself above ground. You would be lucky to see it, however, because the fully opened flower lasts for just four days.

The Monster flower's host is most often a type of vine in the grape family

(*Vitaceae*) called *Tetrastigma*, abundant in the Southeast Asian rainforests. In places where the vine hangs down from the trees and trails across the ground, partly covered with soil, tiny buds develop. The buds grow to the size of large, tightly wrapped cabbages over a period of nine months or more. Suddenly, the extraordinary structure unfolds, revealing five huge, fleshy petals around a deep central cup that holds a large, spiky disk on a pedestal.

Foul-smelling flowers

When it first forms, the Monster flower does not have a distinctive perfume. Within a few days, though, it develops a strong, rancid smell, like rotting fish or meat. Indeed, the local people often call it the "Corpse flower." This smell, combined with the bright red color, attracts flies, which are the flower's main pollinators.

Flies visit the male Monster flower and carry pollen grains from it to the female flower stuck to their bodies. They land on the upper surface of the disk in the center of the female flower, then crawl over the edge to the underside, where a thick forest of hairs guides them to the plant's reproductive organs. There, they inadvertently transfer their precious cargo and pollinate the plant.

Once it has been pollinated, the flower is fertilized and produces a rotting fruit, with thousands of tiny reddish-brown seeds embedded in a slimy mass. The fruit is particularly tasty to small rodents such as squirrels and tree shrews. These animals feed on the fleshy fruit and then distribute the seeds far from the parent plant by carrying them in their fur or paws, or

depositing them in their droppings. Seeds may also be picked up on the hooves of deer or pigs and then trampled into cracks in the host vine. Then the seeds are free to germinate and become a parasite on another vine root.

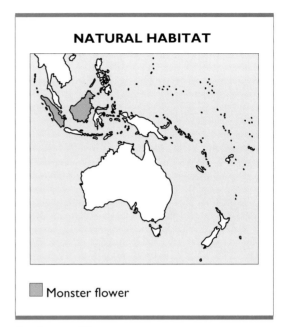

NATURAL HABITAT

☐ Monster flower

Meet the family

The Monster flower and other *Rafflesia* species belong to a group of around 50 different species, found in tropical and subtropical regions of Central and South America, East Africa, South Africa, the Mediterranean, and Southeast Asia. These plants are all parasites, and include the genus *Mitrastemma*. One species of *Mitrastemma* produces "fairy rings," much in the same way as mushrooms and toadstools do, around the roots of its host.

▼ *The Monster flower produces a flower bud (below) about a year and a half after it starts growing on the host vine.*

Rainforest

◄ **The tallest trees form a canopy over the thousands of animals and plants that live below.**

KEY FACTS

● **Location**
Tropical rainforests are found in parts of South America, Africa, Southeast Asia, and Australia

● **Largest**
The largest tropical rainforest is in the Amazon Basin in South America

● **Climate**
Warm and wet, with about 60 in (150 cm) of rain a year; it rains almost every day

● **Abundance**
Tropical rainforests contain an estimated two to three million animal species, two thirds of all forms of life on earth. Most of these are insects

● **Tropical rainforest animals**
Anacondas, anteaters, apes, bats, boas, flying squirrels, monkeys, parrots, porcupines, sloths, tamarins, toucans, tree shrews

---

Rainforests are home to thousands of plants and animals. These forests are rich in nutrients and provide many different habitats in which plants and animals thrive.

There are two types of rainforests: tropical and temperate. Tropical rainforests are found in the area between the Tropic of Cancer and the Tropic of Capricorn. Temperatures and rainfalls are high in these regions all year round. There are tropical rainforests in Southeast Asia, in northeastern Australia, and in Africa. The largest tropical rainforest is the Amazon Basin in central South America.

Tropical rainforests are by far the most common, but there are also temperate rainforests. These occur along the northwest coast of North America where there are moderate temperatures and high rainfall. The largest temperate rainforest, the Tongass National Forest, Alaska, is as big as the state of West Virginia. Most trees here are conifers, such as Douglas firs and Coast redwoods. Vines and ferns hang from the trees, and the forest floor is a mass of mosses, which soak up water like sponges. Deer, elks, squirrels, and many birds and insects live here, too.

The various types and locations of tropical rainforests mean that while some animals and plants are found in all rainforests, there are also variations from place to place. For instance, there are primates (apes and monkeys) in both the Amazon Basin and in Africa, but the species (kinds) are different. The Amazon Basin is particularly known for its vast range of bird species and freshwater fish.

Animals of the rainforest

A huge number of animals live in tropical rainforests. Most of these are insects, but there are many bird and mammal species too. There are few large land animals, however, since dense vegetation makes it difficult for them to move around.

Many tropical rainforest animals have a particularly striking appearance, such as the neotropical American butterfly (*Morpho* spp.), which is metallic blue and can have a wingspan of up to 8 in (20 cm).

Most animals are nocturnal – they sleep during the day and are active at night. Nocturnal rainforest inhabitants include bats, small cats, and mouse deer. These species rely on keen senses of smell and hearing while they forage at night. The darkness helps hide these animals from predators. There are a few species, such as apes and squirrels, that are diurnal (active during the day). Larger animals, such as wild dogs and cats, are active at dusk and at dawn.

Plants

Tropical rainforests are able to support so many animal species because the plants provide such a variety of habitats. The forest canopy covers all the plant life above ground level and the area within this canopy can be split into five levels. Because these levels are at different heights from the ground, the amount of shade at each level varies and attracts different species of plants and animals.

To survive in these dense forests plant species have adapted in different ways. Some are very shade-tolerant so they can grow with little sunlight. Others grow

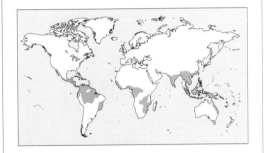

NATURAL HABITAT

■ Tropical rainforest

quickly when gaps appear in the canopy: if, for example, a tree dies. These are called pioneer species, and they are the first to grow in new clearings.

Plants in the lower levels have larger leaves to give a greater surface area for photosynthesis since they receive less light. The tall trees in rainforests may have large roots, called buttresses, that grow above the ground to support them.

Another group of plants found in rainforests are epiphytes such bromeliads and orchids. Epiphytes grow on trees without damaging them.

Use and abuse

Rainforests are the source of many products such as nuts, fruits, and some plants and fungi that provide ingredients for medicines.

▼ A Scarlet macaw is caught in mid-flight. Macaws, which are the largest kind of parrot, thrive on the plentiful nuts and fruit of the rainforest.

THE LEVELS OF THE RAINFOREST

The highest level (the emergent layer) is made up of trees called emergents that reach about 130 ft (40 m) from the ground. Species such as mahogany make up this layer, and their trunks may be covered with creepers or vines. Animals in this layer include bushbabies, flying foxes, and macaws.

This layer of the forest (the upper canopy) is made up of the tops of trees that reach a maximum of about 100 ft (30 m). There are many gaps between the trees. Animals that live in this layer include chameleons, flying squirrels, langurs, and pythons.

This level (the lower canopy) is made up of trees that are 16 to 65 ft (5 to 20 m) tall. These trees are closely packed together and contain most of the animal life, including chimpanzees, orangutans, and tree frogs.

Vegetation at this level (the shrub layer) consists of saplings, shrubs, palms, and tall herbs. Animals that inhabit the shrub layer include squirrels and wild dogs and cats.

The lowest level (the forest floor) consists of ground level plants that receive hardly any light so there are not many of them.

However, wood is the main product harvested. The best known is teak (*Tecona grandis*), which is particularly valued for being hard-wearing.

Unfortunately overharvesting of the wood has been a major contributing factor leading to the destruction of over half the area of tropical rainforests. The forests are also cleared to provide space for farmland. Trees are not only felled for farms but also for roads to allow access to the farms. This in turn gives access to more forest, bringing more people, which leads to further clearance.

This large-scale felling destroys the habitat, leaving plants and animals with nowhere to live. It is leading to the extinction of many species.

Global warming

Logging also has serious effects on the global climate. The dense rainforest vegetation absorbs a lot of energy from the sun. With a reduction in rainforests there is a reduction in their capacity to absorb this energy, leading to changes in regional climates.

Plants also absorb carbon dioxide. This is one of the main gases in the atmosphere that prevents heat escaping from the earth. Therefore with more carbon dioxide in the atmosphere, less heat is able to escape and our planet becomes hotter. This process is called global warming. It is part of what is known as the greenhouse effect, because carbon monoxide traps heat just as the glass of a greenhouse does.

The rainfall within rainforests is mostly the result of water being recycled by the vegetation. A lot of the rainwater taken up by plants evaporates from the surfaces of the leaves. This forms clouds of water vapor, which then fall again as rain. This recycled water may fall back in the forest or, as in the Amazon Basin, it may be blown inland where it falls over the Andes. Rain absorbed into the soil also finds its way into rivers. Less vegetation means less water recycling, which leads to a reduction in rainfall and a drop in water levels of inland lakes and rivers.

For all these reasons, the destruction of rainforests is a major cause for concern. Not only are we losing an important and spectacular habitat for many species of plants and animals, but the effects on our planet as a whole may be severe.

▼ *A young gorilla chews on a tasty plant stem. The few gorillas that survive live in the rainforests of central Africa.*

See also **Anteater, Bird-of-paradise flower, Gibbon, Macaw, Moss, Rubber tree, Sloth, Toucan**

Rat

Rats are large rodents that are very closely related to mice. As with the mice there are some rat species that make their homes in or near human communities, and these are often unpopular and considered pests by many people. The two species most frequently found living alongside humans belong to the same group of mouse-like rodents as the common House mouse – the Old World rats and mice (the *Murinae*). These two species are the Common or Brown rat (also called the Norway rat) and the Roof or Black rat (also called the Ship rat).

Both the Common rat and the Roof rat are found in most parts of the world. Hundreds of years ago they spread from Asia through Europe and from there to North America and other parts of the world. In general, however, the Common rat is most numerous in the world's temperate regions, in country areas as well as in cities. In tropical regions it lives mainly in large cities and ports. The Roof or Black rat is more successful in the tropics, particularly in towns and villages. On tropical islands in the Pacific, Caribbean, and Atlantic, it is also found in the wild and among agricultural crops.

Similar but different

In spite of the fact that the Common and Roof rats are also known as the "brown" and "black" rats, they are very similar in color. The Black rat can be dark brown, and the Brown rat can be black. (Because of this many people prefer to call these

two species by the names Common rat and Roof rat.) However, the two do differ in size and shape.

The Common rat is bigger than the Roof rat. The average size is $9\frac{1}{4}$ in (23 cm) from its nose to the base of its tail, although some may grow up to 10 in (25 cm). Its tail is shorter than its body, and its ears are about one third as long as its head. The Roof rat is not only smaller but also more slender. The average length of the head and body is $7\frac{1}{2}$ in (18.7 cm). The tail, which is about 10 in (25 cm) long, is slimmer than the Common rat's

▲ *This Common rat (Rattus norvegicus) is showing its agility and excellent climbing skills as it scales a pole. This species is also known as the Brown rat.*

▶ *Common rats are extremely successful breeders. These baby rats have a leafy nest in a log pile.*

and almost hairless. The ears are naked and more than half as long as the head.

Enormous appetites

The range of the Common rat in the New World extends from Alaska south as far as the old whaling station of South Georgia on the fringes of the Antarctic. Its rapid spread throughout the world in the eighteenth century was in part a result of the increase in trade between Europe and North and South America. Like the Roof rat, it followed grains and other foods that were being loaded on board ship and so made its way across the world's oceans.

Like most other Old World rats and mice, the Common rat eats a mixture of animal and plant foods, but it eats more meat than most other species. It is well known as a raider of chicken coops and will even steal hen's eggs, although exactly how it manages to carry the eggs away is unknown. The Common rat has an enormous appetite and, when kept in captivity, it needs up to one third its weight in food every day. If a man weighing 180 lb (81.6 kg) were to eat the same amount of food, he would consume 60 lb (27 kg) of food daily.

White rats that are kept as pets or used for scientific research are Common rats that are specially bred from albino forms. (An albino animal lacks the natural pigments that give color to skin, hair, and eyes.) White rats make good pets and are cleaner and easier to keep than mice.

Pack rats

Rats that are native to North America include the wood rats, which are related to the voles and lemmings. In some areas they are popularly known as pack rats because of their habit of bringing objects back to their nests. They are especially attracted to bright-colored or metallic objects. In many cases pack rats will leave another object in the place of the one they have "stolen." For example, they have been known to leave stones in place of metal nuts they have taken.

KEY FACTS

● **Name**
Common, Brown, or Norway rat
(*Rattus norvegicus*)

● **Range**
Worldwide, preferring temperate climates

● **Habitat**
Farm buildings, warehouses, grain elevators, and similar buildings; garbage dumps, river banks, woodlands, and farmland where food crops, especially grains, are grown

● **Appearance**
Head and body up to 10 in (25 cm), with a slightly shorter tail; brown to blackish, or gray, shaggy fur

● **Food**
A wide variety of animal and vegetable food, including a high proportion of grain; it also feeds on root crops; sometimes may steal ducklings or chickens and their eggs

● **Breeding**
The female bears 3-4 litters a year, each with 4-10 young; the young leave the nest at 3 weeks

● **Status**
Common

Rattlesnake

To anyone who knows the open plains of North America, the rattling that the rattlesnake makes as it moves through the scrub is a terrifying sound. Although their venom is not the most poisonous in the world, it can kill a human even when antivenom drugs are available. The Western diamondback is responsible for more serious snakebites and deaths than any other North American snake.

Rattlesnakes (including sidewinders) are members of the viper family. The 30 different species are only found in the Americas, from southern Canada to northern Argentina.

Hunting and feeding

Most rattlesnakes, whether they live on the plains or in more tropical and upland habitats, prey on small mammals and birds. They hunt mainly at night, creeping about silently in search of rabbits, rats, and ground squirrels. In order to kill their prey they sink their front fangs into the victim's body, stabbing rather than biting, and inject it with venom. The venom is one of the most virulent of all venoms and will kill a small rodent in seconds.

Each fang has a series of replacement fangs behind it and when a replacement fang reaches full size, the old fang loosens at its base as the new one moves into position. Unlike humans, who only have two sets of teeth, snakes' fangs are replaced throughout their lives.

The poison paralyses the victim so that the snake can swallow it — headfirst. Seeing a snake swallow a whole animal is an extraordinary sight. Because it cannot hold the victim steady while it bites into it and has no claws to tear it apart, it simply opens its mouth as wide as it can and moves forward with jerking movements, gradually consuming its prey.

▲ *The Western diamondback is a rattler to be feared. Its front fangs are hollow tubes, and when it strikes it sinks its fangs into its victim so it can inject its venom. Then it opens its jaws so wide that it can swallow its prey in one piece.*

Rattling away

The rattle of a rattlesnake is thought to be a defensive measure rather than part of its method of catching prey. The rattle consists of a series of hollow rings at the end of the tail made of the same sort of substance as human fingernails. Young rattlesnakes are born with a single section of their rattle and a new segment is added every time they shed their skins. However, the number of rings in a rattle is no guide to a snake's age, as the end segments of the rattle gradually break off.

If the snake shakes its tail, these horny segments strike against each other making a buzzing sound. It is usually thought that the loud buzz it produces is a warning to scare off predators. Another theory is that it makes any predator turn to the snake's tail rather than its more vulnerable head. This gives the snake the chance to strike while the predator's attention is distracted.

Social life

Most of the time, rattlesnakes hide in the scrub and undergrowth, hunting or digesting their prey. In cold weather, in

NATURAL HABITAT

☐ Western diamondback rattlesnake

▲ *This prairie rattlesnake has the typical dusty beige coloring of the family. Its rattle shows clearly, poking through the coils of its body.*

the northern part of their range, however, large numbers gather together to hibernate over the winter. They huddle together in pits, only emerging again in the spring. In some parts of the United States there are "rattlesnake round-ups," and vast numbers of hibernating rattlers are killed at a time.

During the breeding season, male rattlers can be seen fighting each other. They coil themselves around each other in a wrestling match, but they have never been known to bite each other.

These snakes are unusual in that the young are born live rather than hatching from eggs as most snakes do. However, once they are born the female usually moves away from them and leaves the young snakes to fend for themselves.

Small cousins

One group of rattlesnakes, the pygmy rattlesnakes, prefer the warm, moist and swampy lands of central and northern South America, where they feed on amphibians and fish.

KEY FACTS

● **Name**
Western diamondback rattlesnake (*Crotalus atrox*)

● **Range**
Central Arkansas and Texas to southeastern California, south into parts of Mexico

● **Habitat**
Dry or semiarid, brushy plains; canyons; hillsides; high semitropical forest areas

● **Appearance**
30-72 in (76-183 cm) long; variable color, brown or gray, sometimes with red or yellow tones; diamond-shaped blotches, usually darker than the body color; the tail is strongly ringed with black and white or light gray; may have dusty appearance

● **Food**
Rabbits and rodents

● **Breeding**
Up to 24 young in late summer or early fall; the young are 10-14 in (25-36 cm) long at birth, with a sharply defined diamond pattern

● **Status**
Widespread

See also **Viper, Sidewinder**

Raven

◄ *Ravens often build their nests on high cliffs. The nest has a deep cup in the center lined with bark, animal hair, wool, mosses, grasses, lichens, or even seaweed. This is the female sitting on the nest to keep the eggs warm. She remains there for 18-20 days, during which time the male feeds her.*

The Common raven is the largest member of the crow family – indeed it has the largest body of all the songbirds or perching birds. There are 10 different species of raven altogether, of which two species, the Common raven and the smaller Chihuahuan raven (*Corvus cryptoleucus*) of the southwestern states, are found in North America.

Adaptable lifestyle

Ravens are long-lived birds that are renowned for their intelligence. The fact that they are crafty and quick to learn means that they have been able to adapt to changes in the environment brought about by humans. For example, part of their food comes from scavenging. In the past they had to compete with other animals in wild habitats for the meat of animals that had died or been abandoned by other predators. Now they have learned that they can often find dead animals along highways and freeways, and they also follow plows for grubs turned up by farmers. They have to compete with gulls and vultures for some of their food.

Another sign of their intelligence is the way they tackle crustaceans and mollusks. They pick up the shellfish and drop them from a height onto a rock so that the cases crack and they can get at the food inside. When food is plentiful they hide their surplus for leaner times.

Ravens have found they can live in a wide range of "wilderness" habitats, from the treeless tundra in the north, through temperate forests and mountainous terrain

► *The raven is a large bird with a huge, black, slightly downward-curving beak. Its deep, croaking call is a well-known sound in many parts of the world.*

NATURAL HABITAT

☐ Common raven

to the desert regions, but they have also learned to occupy quarries and buildings.

Stable partnerships

Ravens pair up together for life. In some parts of the world the birds migrate toward the equator during the winter months, but many birds remain in the area near their nests for the whole year. They are generally solitary birds, but at certain times of year pairs of birds can be seen diving and soaring together like falcons, or somersaulting and circling for hours like eagles. These spectacular flights usually occur at the end of the winter, and scientists think that they are pairs meeting up together after spending the winter months alone. Other scientists suggest that the flights are simply a form of play.

When they have paired up, the ravens work hard to build a nest. They choose a cliff, a treetop, or even a building and construct a nest from twigs and branches. The pair do not collect the material from the ground, but always use sticks that they have broken off trees. Even if they accidentally drop one of their twigs, they do not pick it up from the ground but snap off another to replace it.

KEY FACTS

● **Name**
Common or American raven (*Corvus corax*)

● **Range**
Eurasia, North and Central America

● **Habitat**
Tundra, coastal regions, riverbanks, rocky cliffs, forests, plains, and deserts

● **Appearance**
$21\frac{1}{2}$-27 in (54-68 cm) long, with a wingspan of 46-56 in (115-140 cm); all black with a lustre of purple and green; a large black bill; a long tail that looks wedge-shaped in flight; the male is larger than the female

● **Food**
Carrion (dead mammals and fish); worms, reptiles, shellfish, the eggs and young of other birds

● **Breeding**
Large nest built on cliffs or in trees; 3-7 eggs are laid in March-June; both parents feed the young; 1 brood per year

● **Status**
Widespread; common in some parts of its range

See also **Crow**

Ray

Rays are strange-looking flat fish. Most of the 300 species in the world live on the seabed in warm oceans. Some live in fresh water, and one group, the manta rays, are found in deeper waters, close to the surface. Rays are part of the order of fish known as cartilaginous: instead of having a bony skeleton, they have a skeleton made of cartilage (like the flexible "bone" in a human's nose). Cartilage is lighter, softer and more elastic than bone, helping to make the fish surprisingly agile.

Rays are related to sharks; indeed they are sometimes described as flat sharks. The terms skate and ray are often used interchangeably. Sometimes the name skate is used for larger species of ray, or for species with longer snouts. They all have flat bodies that extend sideways into large rounded or pointed fins. They swim by gently rippling the long edges of their fins. They have long, thin whip-like tails, that do not serve any useful purpose.

On the seabed

Because many species of ray live on the ocean floor, their backs are usually colored to camouflage them against the sand and rocks, while their undersides are pale. This pale coloring helps to disguise the species that swim in open ocean from predators that might attack from below. Any creatures that do attack rays have to be able to bite into the rough, scaly, and spiny skin that is a feature of most species.

Because rays are flat, their gills are tucked away on the underside of the body and their eyes are on the top of the body;

KEY FACTS

- **Name**
  Atlantic manta ray
  or devilray
  (*Manta birostris*)

- **Range**
  Tropical and warm
  temperate parts of
  Atlantic Ocean

- **Habitat**
  Surface waters of
  shallow and open sea

- **Appearance**
  Up to 17 ft (5.2 m)
  long and 22 ft (6.7 m)
  wide; dark olive to
  black, with a pale
  underside; a broad,
  flat "body" with
  powerful pectoral
  fins; a long tail

- **Food**
  Plankton, small fish,
  crustaceans

- **Breeding**
  Bear live young

- **Status**
  Widespread

in many species the eyes are protected by fleshy bumps, while in others they are just flat openings in the top of the head. Their mouths are also on the underside of the body so they can feed on the seabed.

Small food

Although some rays are quite large fish, all feed on small organisms. Those that live in shallow water scrape fish, mollusks, and crustaceans from the ocean floor, crushing the shells in their mouths. In open oceans manta rays are filter feeders, sifting plankton and small fish out of the water through special gill openings as they swim along, in a similar way to Blue whales. They only take very small organisms, as they do not have a large enough mouth or sharp enough teeth for large prey.

Another unusual feature of rays is that in many species the females bear live young, another feature that they share with sharks. In most species of fish, the female lays eggs that are then fertilized by the male outside her body. In the case of the rays, the male holds the female close with special claspers on the underside of the body so that he can pass sperm to her. She then gives birth to a small number of live young. In those species of ray where the young are not born live, the female lays a small number of fertilized eggs in a strong, horn-like capsule.

Harmless and harmful

The largest of the rays, the Atlantic manta, with its huge, pointed fins, is a harmless species, and stories of it drowning swimmers by wrapping them in its fins are exaggerated. However, some

rays are not so friendly. There are more than 30 species of electric ray, which are found in tropical and subtropical seas. They have rounded bodies, smooth skin, and short tails. They are slow swimmers and live on the ocean bed in shallow waters. Here they catch their prey (other fish) by wrapping them in their fins and stunning them with electric shocks. The shocks are produced by special organs at the bases of their pectoral fins. The largest electric ray is the Atlantic torpedo ray (*Torpedo nobiliana*), which grows to over 6 ft (2 m).

Another family of rays with a poor reputation is the stingray family. There are about 100 different species, in tropical and subtropical oceans (although two South American groups live in fresh water). They have spines with venom sacs at the base of their tail. Although the venom is not always fatal to humans, in the past many deaths have been caused due to the wound getting infected.

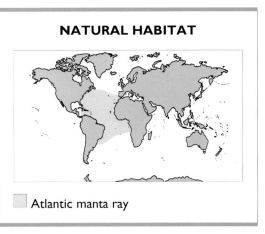

NATURAL HABITAT

Atlantic manta ray

▼ *This Yellow stingray, well disguised against the sandy floor of the Caribbean sea, has a sting in its tail. If a human steps on the spines around its tail, the result is very painful. The barbs on the spines lodge in the skin and make them very difficult to remove. Tail spines of stingrays are sold as souvenirs, often in the form of letter-openers.*

See also **Shark**

Index

Page numbers in **boldface type** show full articles

J
578
WIL

AUG   2006

Wildlife and Plants of the
    World V.12